Amish Knitting Circle Christmas

Granny & Jeb's Love Story

KAREN ANNA VOGEL

He Restores My Soul

Amish Knitting Circle Christmas: Granny & Jeb's Love Story

© 2012 by Karen Anna Vogel

Second Edition 2013 by Lamb Books

All rights reserved. No part of this publication may be reproduced, stored in a retrieval system, or transmitted by any means – electronic, mechanical, photographic (photocopying), recording, or otherwise – without prior permission in writing from the author.

This book is a work of fiction. The names, characters, places, and incidents are products of the writer's imagination or have been used fictitiously and are not to be construed as real. Any resemblance to persons, living or dead, actual events, locales or organizations is entirely coincidental.

Contact the author on Facebook at: www.facebook.com/VogelReaders

Learn more the author at: www.karenannavogel.com

Visit her blog, Amish Crossings, at www.karenannavogel.blogspot.com

ISBN-13:978-0615910741 (Lamb Books)

ISBN-10:0615910742

Dedication

This book is dedicated to my dad, John Bolkovac, who embodied the spirit of Christmas. Who else goes on an icy roof to mount a plastic Santa and his reindeer, giving off enough light to challenge a full-moon? So, when he passed away on Christmas Day, 1996, it was hard to understand. But I kept hearing at the funeral home, "He went home for Christmas." I chose to believe that, too. No more pain and suffering was a gift God gave my dad for Christmas.

I still miss you Daddy. Especially when I see department store trees decorated in 1960s ornaments. They're back in style!

CONTENTS

	Prologue ~A Christmas Party	1
1	*Back to 1963*	7
2	*Jeb leaves the Allegheny Mountains*	21
3	*Road Less Taken*	35
4	*Granny Leaves Millersburg, Ohio*	47
5	*Not Love at First Sight!*	61
6	*Granny's Leaving the Amish?*	79
7	*Change of Heart*	95
8	*Staying Amish!*	109
9	*Thanksgiving*	123
10	*Jingle Bells!*	137
11	*Sparks Fly*	149
12	*Love?*	159
13	*Two Candles Shine Brighter*	171
14	*A Merry Christmas*	181
15	*Wedding Plans*	187
	Dear Readers, Recipes & Whatnot	191

Karen Anna Vogel

Amish – English Dictionary

Ach – Oh
Boppli – Baby
Bruder – Brother
Daed – Dad
Dochder – Daughter
Furhoodled – Mixed-Up
Gmay – Church/
Guder Mariye- Good Morning
Gut – Good
Jah – Yes
Kapp – Prayer Cap Used by Amish Women to Cover Their Head
Kinner – Children or Grandchildren
Mamm – Mom Nee – No
Okey Dokey – Okay
Oma – Grandma
Opa – Grandpa
Ordnung – German word for order. A set of rules for Amish living, but can vary from each church district.
Rumspringa – Running around time for Amish teens
Swartzentruber Amish – Strictest Amish sect
Wunderbar – Wonderful

Prologue

A Christmas Party

Granny rubbed her hands together, creating warmth, even though the woodstove and cook stove were blazing forth heat. Such a cold snap reminded her of the buggy ride Jeb took her on when they started courting.

"Granny, are you alright?" Fannie asked, putting an arm around her back. "You're flushed."

"Just thinking…"

"Now don't worry. We have all the cookie's ready on the trays and the girls are in the living room knitting. Ella's pouring coffee."

Granny turned to embrace the girl that had become like a daughter…like she was to her Aunt Mary. "Fannie, I love you so."

Fannie slowly pulled her away, and looked deeply into her eyes. "What's wrong? Tell me? You sick, aren't you?"

"What?"

"Your face is red and now you're not talking like yourself. You show me you love me all the time."

Granny's eyes misted. "Like I said, just thinking. Christmas brings back memories…"

"Of what?"

"Well, every year it's something else. But this year, I'm thinking about my move to Smicksburg, back in 1963. I met Jeb here, you know."

Fannie cocked an eyebrow. "You didn't know him in Ohio?"

"*Nee*, he' not from Ohio. He was a mountain man from the Allegheny Mountains."

Fannie chuckled. "*Ach*, don't pull my leg."

"I'm not." Granny lifted a tray of ginger cookies and headed toward the living room, a few steps from her kitchen, now that she lived in *a dawdyhaus*. "Who has a sweet tooth?"

"I do," Lizzie and Ruth said in unison, laughter filling the room afterward.

Granny placed the cookies on the new coffee table Jeb built her for her Christmas. "Now, how many socks do we have to pack up this year?"

Maryann sat in an Amish rocker near a large box. "One hundred-fifty pairs. We'll have to make more, don't you think?"

"*Jah*, a lot more," Ella said, as she continued to knit the pair of black socks she was working on. "

"Well, we have all winter to knit for the homeless," Fannie chimed in. "But I think Granny has a telling to give us."

Granny put a hand up. "Christmas just floods my mind with memories is all. At seventy, I have more than two or three of you young folk combined."

"Granny, tell us about Jeb being a mountain man, unless it really was a joke," Fannie blurted, as she looked around the circle. "I kind of think it's true. Is it?"

"*Jah*, and when we met, sparks did fly." Ella put her knitting down. "I felt that way when I met Zach. I knew he was the one I'd wed."

"*Ach*, not Jeb and me. Sparks flew due to…friction. It's a long story and this is our Christmas cookie and boxing party. Need to get everything packed so we won't have to pay priority shipping."

Granny sat down and picked up her knitting. The wind howled and tree branches cracked, and that was the only sound. After a few seconds, she looked up. "Is something wrong?"

All eyes were fixed on her, and she shifted in her chair.

"What?"

"Are you going to tell the story?" Ruth asked. "It would be a real treat if you did."

Granny looked into Ruth's dark brown eyes. Did she need more advice concerning her marriage? How to work problems out? "Well, you may find it boring, but if you want me to I can."

The girls all nodded, urging her on.

"Well, to get the whole story straight, I should ask Jeb to come on out and tell his side."

"His side?" Ella asked. "You make it sound like more of a quarrel than a love story."

"That is was, at first." Granny yelled out into the kitchen. "Jeb, come on out. I know you're in there trying to find stray cookies."

"I am not," Jeb's voice resounded throughout the house. "Just getting hot chocolate made."

"*Nee*, you're looking for cookies like you do every year. Can you come out here?"

"Why?"

"They want to hear our love story."

"Why?"

"Old man, come in here, or I'll tell it all from my point of view."

Soon Jeb was seen coming in the living room, a red plaid blanket wrapped around him for extra warmth. "*Ach*, now, I do need to be here then. She might exaggerate at my expense."

Granny kept looking down as she knit. "You want to go first?"

Jeb plunked himself in a chair. "*Nee*, you can start. Your part is more…well…surprising."

Chapter 1

Back to 1963

Deborah stared across the oak table, shoulders firm. "*Jah, Daed.* I said no."

She jumped when he pounded the table, sorry that once again he'd been disappointed.

"You're twenty-one. How could you?"

Measuring her breath, Deborah said what she always did when turning down a marriage proposal. "I don't love him." Why couldn't her *daed* see that love was in the equation? Not wanting to marry and see if love bloomed eventually, she wanted to say her vows from the heart…one filled with joy at a union.

"You're *furhoodled*, Deborah," her *mamm* said wearily. "Marriage is a commitment. Maybe tell Noah that you've changed your mind."

Deborah dipped her gaze into the blue and white China cup. The chamomile tea she'd made wasn't calming her nerves any. Neither was the cup given to her by her *oma*...the rest of the set was in her hope chest. *Jah*, her *oma* had great hopes too, and made it a monthly ritual to crochet a doily or sew a pot holder to add to the cedar chest that sat at the foot of her bed - her *daed* made the chest.

"*Mamm. Daed.* There isn't anyone in the *Gmay* I could see spending my life with. But I'm not unhappy."

Her father pounded the table again. "Spinster... indeed. All you want to do is spin wool."

Deborah contributed to the household budget by selling yarn, so she didn't feel she was a burden. And she shouldered so many chores, since all her brothers were married and living on their own farms, spread out across Millersburg, Ohio.

"Smicksburg," her *mamm* said evenly. "There's a new settlement in Smicksburg. I think you should go live with your Aunt Mary and Uncle Isaac."

Deborah's eyes darted to meet her *mamm*'s. "*Nee.* I belong here."

"You need a husband," her *daed* boomed. "And quick. You're getting older…"

Her mother came and sat next to her, rubbing her back. "What your *daed* is saying is that those light blue eyes of yours are getting crow's feet."

"They're laugh lines, *Mamm*. It's because I don't take life so seriously and *laugh*, that I have those lines. Plus, I do my share in the outside work in the hot sun…with *daed*. I get dry skin."

The autumn wind shook the windows, and Deborah looked out to see the many-colored leaves fly off the large maple tree. "I belong here. My roots are here." She put her hand over her face as if to build a fortress around herself.

"Either tell Noah you've been *furhoodled* and changed your mind, or settle in Smicksburg."

Her *daed*'s voice wasn't his usual jovial tone, and he looked pale and sickly. Was he really that worried about her? If so, she'd have to ease his burden. "Can I think about this for a few days?"

"So, you'll talk with Noah, *jah*?" her *mamm* chimed in. "I knew you cared for him."

Deborah shook her head. "*Nee*, just about moving to Smicksburg."

Crows cawed outside, and several blackbirds settled in the maple tree. The tree that she'd planted with her *daed* when a wee one. He dug the hole and let her set the sapling in place. Now he was out of breath after hand milking a few cows. "*Daed*, you need me here to milk."

"I'll get help." He pushed away from the table and stood up. "You can't be my shadow forever...as much as I'd like that." He opened his arms and Deborah ran around the table and flew into them. "Sorry for my temper. I do love my *dochder*. I'm grieved is all."

"You really like Noah, don't you?" Deborah asked.

"*Jah*. He's a fine young man..."

"He's, well...boring."

Her *mamm* got up to clear the table. "But he's an agreeable man."

"That's the problem. He agrees with everything I say. If I said Amish men should wear bell bottoms, he'd agree!"

Her *daed* gripped her tighter around the shoulders. "I'll have no talk of these new English styles."

"I'm sorry, *Daed*. That wasn't a *gut* example."

"*Nee*, it wasn't," her *mamm* added for emphasis. "You haven't been friendly with any English or ones that have strayed…shunned… have you? You are a baptized member of the church."

Deborah felt like cold water from the outside pump had been splashed in her face. Her *rumspringa* was over, for sure and for certain. And so were her ties to Samuel. How could her *mamm* even elude to him? She was being treated like a teenager…maybe it was time to move on…

~*~

Jeb pulled up the buggy robe as the mountain air grew colder. Coming out of the Allegheny Mountains to the foothills, as he headed towards Smicksburg, he hoped it would be warmer, but a brisk wind blew right through him. Doubts plagued his mind. Was the new settlement any different than the strict Swartzentruber sect he'd just left? Were his *bruder's* letters exaggerated? Well, he was the last one to leave, finding no reason to stay after his parents' deaths. Except for Sarah, but that was over.

He flicked the reins to pick up speed to keep in pace with his racing mind. How could the girl he'd grown up with, gone to the same one-room schoolhouse with, courted since sixteen, refuse to see his point of view? Maybe what bothered him was that he was afraid she was right; having a lantern at the same height on both sides of his wagon showed pride. Just like having two matching suspenders; he should only have one strap going up his back, since two that matched was forbidden. His brother, Abe, had sent him the two strapped suspenders to give him a taste of Smicksburg, and freedom.

As he rounded the corner of the windy road, he saw a black man with a red checkered knapsack over his shoulder. Had his car broken down? The man simply turned and stuck out his thumb. Was he pointing at something? He pulled the buggy over to a clearing. "Can I help you?"

The man ran over to the buggy. "Thanks, man." He hopped into the buggy and sat next to Jeb. "You headed towards Pittsburgh?"

"Smicksburg," Jeb said, shocked that an Englisher would want to ride in a buggy. "I can take you that far."

"I appreciate it, even though it may take a week."

"*Nee*, we'll be there by nightfall." Jeb glanced over at the man beside him. He seemed a bit on edge. Most likely was afraid of being in a buggy on a busy road. "Haven't had an accident yet."

"What?"

"The buggy. It's safe."

"I'd rather be in an Amish buggy than be picked up by some whites right now."

Jeb shook his head. "I'm white."

"You don't know, do you?"

Jeb scratched his clean-shaven chin. "About what?"

"The marches and protests. Blacks are going to be equal with Whites, soon. Same schools, same everything."

"I agree, and I do know something about prejudice, too."

"Now how would you know anything about how my people suffer? You're as white as they come."

Jeb held up his thermos. "Thirsty?"

"Huh?"

"You said I don't know anything, right? Well, I do. Your people can't drink from public fountains…and I'm a shunned man."

"Really? What did you do?"

Jeb was used to ridicule but it didn't stop the sting, so be braced himself as he told this stranger the reason for his shunning. "I wore suspenders with two straps…"

The man took the thermos and slid the lid off. "That's strange, but people can pick the stupidest things to argue about."

No mockery was in his voice, to Jeb's relief. "I know. That's how I see it. We have too much in the Bible to agree on, so why spend time knit-pickin' about little things."

"And they're no suspenders in the Bible." The man nudged Jeb with his elbow and snickered. "I'm Carl. What's your name?"

"Jebediah Weaver."

"Nice to meet you." He held up the thermos. "Are you sure I can drink from this?"

"*Jah*, I'm sure."

"So, do you have family in Smicksburg?"

"A *bruder* and his wife. Do you have family in Pittsburgh?"

"I'm from down South. Was up in New York, but headed to Pittsburgh for a march. Ever hear of Martin Luther?"

"*Ach, jah*, we Amish are Protestant, and we go back a long way back to Luther."

Carl slapped his knee and roared. "Man, that was a good one. No, seriously, have you heard of Martin Luther? Martin Luther King?"

Jeb angled his head, confused.

"Well, he's a Baptist minister who's peacefully standing up for our rights as black folk. I hitch a ride to as many of his marches as I can."

Jeb pulled into a little country restaurant. "As long as your marches are peaceful, it sounds like a *gut* thing. Hungry?" Jeb jumped out of the buggy and was grieved to see Carl's countenance fall and shame spread across his face. "What's wrong?"

"I have food in my knap sack. You go ahead on in."

"It's cold out here. Come in."

"It's full of whites here. And the KKK is active in these parts, from what I hear."

Jeb knew what the KKK was. As he saw fear creep into Carl's eyes, righteous anger threatened to boil up from within. "Such a shame. I'll get you a hot sandwich and bring it out?"

Carl held Jeb's probing eyes. "Thanks, man. You're really cool."

"Cool? I'm freezing," Jeb said, rubbing his hands together for warmth.

~*~

Deborah pulled into her *oma*'s long driveway. When her white house came into view, she once again was breath taken by the colorful plants that adorned her wraparound porch. Burgundy and yellow mums were her *opa*'s favorite, and from this view, she saw what she wanted; a marriage like her *oma* and *opa* enjoyed. Still in love in their old age. Surely there was advice to be unearthed from this couple, and she was on a mission to find it.

When she arrived at the house, the door opened as usual, and her *oma* opened the door and stood on the porch, arms open wide with a smile. Deborah ran to her, but this time not for a loving embrace, but out of great need and distress.

And her *oma* could tell.

"What ails you, Love?"

Deborah clung to her. "I'm so wretched a creature."

"*Ach*, Deborah, speak plainly. What are you reading now?"

She lowered her head. "Little Women."

"Humph. It's not true, you know. Why read something that's not true?"

"*Oma*, I learn a lot. It's like a long parable in the Bible."

"But, it's not the Bible and you know it…"

Deborah sat in one of the rockers on her *oma*'s porch. "Why did you marry *Opa*?"

Her *oma* made her way to the rocker next to her. "He's the only one who asked…"

"*Oma*, you were sixteen. Not much time for courting anyone else."

A grin slipped across her face. "Well, that's true." She put her hands to her heart. "I knew in here."

"How did you know in your heart? As you know, *mamm* wants me to marry Noah…"

"Do you respect him?"

Deborah leaned her head back. "Is it a sin not to respect someone? The Bible says to respect everyone."

"You know what I mean. Let's be honest, we can both say we don't respect Otis, *jah*? Almost put your *daed* in the hospital when he found out he was shouting something fierce at you."

"*Ach*, my *bruders* were fit to be tied, too. But Noah's a much better man than Otis."

"Let me put it another way. When he talks, do you follow his conversation, or in your mind want to change his words, thinking him foolish?"

Deborah put up both hands in surrender. "Change his words. He's too agreeable."

"As if he doesn't have a mind of his own?"

"*Jah*, that's it. And no, I don't respect him for that." Deborah looked over at her *oma*. "You always help me."

"Now hold on. A woman wants to be loved, *jah*? Is that what's bothering you too, concerning Noah?"

"*Jah*, all he talks about is farming."

"A reaction. Look at how he reacts, not acts. Maybe you're missing the signs of love. Your *opa*'s a quiet man and sometimes I need to hear words of love…I read between the lines. You know, wait for his reaction."

"How so?"

"Well, when I'm sick, he fusses over me, bringing me soup. That's his reaction to me being sick, and I see his love, even though he seldom says it.

Deborah pursed her lips, afraid they would start to tremble. She was so close to her *oma*. How could she live so far away? "I'll look for a reaction in Noah. He is a fine man…and I'd hate to leave Millersburg…and you."

Chapter 2

Jeb leaves the Allegheny Mountains

Jebediah lit the lanterns that hung unevenly from either side of the buggy. "We only have a few more miles to go and I'm glad. Low on lantern oil."

"We could have gotten there sooner if it wasn't for me…" Carl's shoulders slouched.

"I might not be alive if I hadn't picked you up. *Danki*, again. Have never been ten miles outside the community. Didn't know there were *Englishers* that liked to test Amish pacifism…"

"Well, I'm not a pacifist. A good thing for both of us."

"But how can you carry a gun?"

"Well, I only take it with me when I think I'm going to be hitchhiking with an Amish man." Carl winked. "And those guys would have beaten you to a pulp."

Jeb put a hand up. "I would have shown them the love of God by turning the other cheek."

Carl rolled his eyes. "Whatever floats your boat, man. But for me, I carry a gun."

Jeb noticed stores ahead, and realized Abe wasn't exaggerating in his letter. The town was small and with little shops for necessities. He noticed two restaurants, but didn't dare go in with Carl, after the encounter with the *Englishers* at the other restaurant; prejudiced against the Amish and Blacks. He had to admit, he was glad he had Carl with him. Not only for protection, but for his camaraderie. Carl knew how he felt: rejected and misunderstood. And definitely not respected, after the shunning.

That Sarah didn't even say good-bye, knowing the sorrow he was trying hard to mask: the death of his parents a year ago. He'd maintained their farm by himself, expecting to fill it with *kinner*. How he longed to farm and teach his sons all he knew about crops and animal husbandry. But when Abe left a few months back, and the letters came in rapid succession, warning him that the *Ordnung* was too strict, he expected Sarah to agree, since he showed her every one of the letters. Sarah only cowered, afraid someone would find out she'd read them. Truth be told, he found her lack of backbone unattractive at time. He needed a woman with a mind of her own, to some degree.

Jeb got the map out of his little suitcase, and glanced at it again. "Looks like we take two rights and my brother's place is the second farm on the left."

"I'll just get out here," Carl said, skittishly.

"*Nee*, you'll stay with us tonight, enjoy a home cooked meal. Maybe stay a few days."

"In a white house? Carl blurted.

"All the Amish have white houses," Jeb said, confused.

"No, man. I mean in a house full of white people."

Jeb patted Carl's back. "It will be fine. You wait and see."

As they made their way to the farm, a brilliant sunset could be seen as they ascended the hill. "The heavens declare the glory of God…"

"…and the firmament sheweth his handiwork." Carl said in a far-off voice. "So many colors."

"*Jah*, and it wouldn't be so majestic if there weren't so many." He knew why his friend was sullen. God made all shades and colors of skin, but why were some deemed inferior? "Looks like we're here," Jeb said as he pulled into his brother's farmhouse. "And, you, my friend, are coming into that big white house."

Carl surprised Jeb by breaking into laughter.

~*~

Deborah took Noah's hand and stepped into the buggy. Being short, it was a challenge, but Noah soon put his hands tenderly on her waist and hoisted her up. Heat filled her cheeks, making them as crimson as some of the leaves on the trees.

Noah's attempts to keep her in Millersburg, she had to admit, were endearing. Showing her the land he bought, that came with a nice barn he said, was calling out for sheep to find a home. *As many as she wanted*, he said. He could picture her spinning wool on the wraparound porch he'd build her, just like her *oma*'s. *Was this love?*

Oh, and he looked so handsome today, his auburn hair more colorful in the sun. And those blue eyes, so big she felt she could jump into them like a fishing hole. His chiseled chin she thought would be a shame to cover with a beard, once married...

As they made their way to the Islay's for a milkshake, something Noah knew was one of her weaknesses; she started to fret. How could she get a reaction out of him? The rattling of the buggy and the whisking of the wind made it hard to hear, but she made an attempt. "Noah, I'm feeling a sore throat come on."

"You can get something hot to drink at Islay's. Hot tea might help."

"*Danki.*" With her *daed* encouraging her to accept, she felt her stomach knot. Why couldn't Noah speak from his heart? She knew she was being impulsive, again, but couldn't help it. "Noah, out of all the girls in Millersburg, why me?" She blurted, hoping for some reaction to an unexpected question.

"No one can cook like you, that's for sure. And you do farm chores like a man."

Deborah's eyes boar through him. "*Ach*, is that so?"

He took her hand. "I'm teasing. You know I'm not *gut* with words. They get caught in here." He pointed to his heart.

He'd said that before…every time she'd prodded him. Out of the abundance of the mouth, the heart speaks, the Good Book said. If he couldn't speak of his feelings, maybe all he did want was a help-mate. She withdrew her hand. "I'd like to go home."

"But you need some hot tea, *jah*?"

"I can make it at home. And I don't have an appetite at all."

He took her hand again. "Let's just talk then…"

Stunned, she slowly looked his way. "Okay. About what?"

"Well, how about the farm I just bought. Isn't that a house any woman would want to live in?"

"*Jah*, if there's love in the home. That's what a woman wants more than a nice house."

He fidgeted nervously with the reins. "My *mamm* said you build love, like you build a barn."

"How so?" Deborah asked.

"One board at a time. After we wed, you can start to build a house full of love, one board at a time."

Deborah's heart sank. How unromantic. Using carpentry terms to describe love? But she promised her *oma* to prod, so she continued. "And what do those boards look like. What are they made of?"

Noah's eyes narrowed, deep in thought. "The Bible says it's the woman's job. Every wise woman builds her house: but the foolish plucks it down with her hands.

She clucked her tongue in disgust and withdrawing her hand, turned from him. Out of the corner of her eye she saw a turquoise colored car, speeding towards the intersection they were about to cross. "Stop!" she yelled.

Noah pulled back on the reins but the horse got skittish and made a dash across the road. They were able to dodge being hit by the car, but the horse was spooked, plowing its way into the nearby field. The tossing and jolting that ensued made Deborah hold on to Noah for dear life.

After a few minutes of mayhem, the horse slowed to a walk, then a halt. Noah jumped out of the buggy and ran to the horse. "There, Daisy. That's a girl. You okay?" He nuzzled his face against the horse's cheek, stroking her black mane as he continued to whisper words of comfort.

Deborah was trembling so much that she had a hard time getting the handkerchief out of her apron pocket to wipe the perspiration off her forehead. *You watch how they react, not act.* The advice her *oma* had given her bolted through her mind. And she didn't know if it was her nerves or something else, but she felt like laughing.

Here was Noah, who acted like he loved her, caring more about the horse's welfare than hers? She'd clung to him, thinking they were facing death, and he never once put his arm around her or tried to calm her. Yes, he had to hold the reins with two hands, but this wasn't the first time she'd been in a buggy with a spooked horse. Her *bruder* or *daed* would say something, even if it was hold on. But, no, Noah said nothing. She would be spending the winter in Smicksburg, visiting her relatives.

~*~

Jeb tried not to stare at all the books his brother had on a long oak shelf in the living room. The Holy Bible was in its rightful place, along with farming books and cookbooks, but he was curious as to the other writers. "Who's Charles Dickens?"

Carl's eyes grew as round as buttons as he slowly looked up from his newspaper. "You're serious?"

"*Jah*, I am."

"He's a writer. An author who really spoke up for the rights of the poor and oppressed."

Jeb scratched his chin. "Like your Martin Luther King, *jah*?"

"Yes sir, like King." Carl winked.

"Then who's Betty Crocker?"

Carl shot a look at Jeb, then the bookshelf. "I see. You're not allowed to read books or something?"

"Back home, in Cambria County, the Bible, *jah*, but not much else. The almanac and farm journals were allowed." He spied his brother coming in from the kitchen. "Did you and Emma have a *gut* Bible reading?"

Abe, tall and lanky, like Jeb, slouched in a rocker next to Carl. "*Nee*, just reading over some letters…from back home."

"So, you have a contact? Who's sticking their neck out?"

Abe fidgeted with the hem of his pant leg, then met Jeb's gaze. "Sarah. She's close with Emma, like you know."

"I know. But we're all shunned. Is she reconsidering? Coming out?"

Abe shrugged his shoulders. "Don't know. Maybe. She's confused."

"About what? The *Ordnung*?"

"*Jah*. She feels it's too strict, too. But, she has her folks to think about…"

Carl leaned forward. "Excuse me for interfering, but your religion seems awfully harsh. Too many do's and don'ts about things that God don't care squat about. God cares about the heart, dig?"

"Dig?" Jeb asked. "What's a *heartdig*? Never heard of that neither."

Carl slapped his leg and laughed. "Jeb, I knew you had a funny bone in you."

Abe twiddled his thumbs while keeping an eye on Carl. "I don't understand what you mean neither."

Carl's eyebrows shot up. "About God caring about the heart? Well, let me explain. He just doesn't care about the color of skin or the type of clothes you wear. He looks into a person's heart and sees what we all know is true, if we had the courage."

Jeb tilt his head. "What?"

"That we're all sinners in need of a savior. We've all missed the mark, man. I mean, get real. No one's perfect except God. We all need a cleansing from the inside, where God's lookin'. Color of skin or clothes don't matter at all."

Abe got out his pipe, lit it, and took a puff. "Carl, we don't wear our clothes different for God to love us."

"Really?" Carl and Jeb asked in unison.

"*Nee*. We wear our clothes to show unity, and to save money."

Carl leaned back. "Martin Luther is a real fan of St. Francis of Assisi. So, you're saying you dress like monks? To not be so concerned about fashion."

"*Jah*," Abe said. "We don't conform to the ways of the world, like St. Francis."

Jeb felt heat rise in his face. "Can't say that I've met Francis."

Carl grinned. "None of us have. He lived 300 years after Christ. He wore a black robe, like all the others who lived with him. He based his life on The Sermon on the Mount."

"Now that's something I do know about…The Sermon on the Mount." Jeb sat up straighter in his rocker.

Carl put his hands behind his head and leaned back, looking deeply satisfied. Jeb had been talking to him over the past few days, and learned more about the Bible and God than all his twenty-three years combined. "Carl, have you ever thought of being a minister?"

Carl grinned. "Can only preach to black folk, and it seems like it's the whites who need the education." He clasped his hand over his mouth. "Oh, I'm sorry. You two don't act like no white folk I've met."

"From what you've told me, that's a *gut* thing," Jeb said, feeling righteous anger again.

"I never knew Amish would be so nice. Since you always wear black and blue, it makes you seem mean."

"Well, we can wear green and burgundy here in Smicksburg."

Jeb couldn't believe what Abe just said. "Green? Burgundy? You know, I thought I saw some women in town wearing green, but I figured they were Mennonite."

"*Nee*, they're Amish. No Mennonites around here, yet."

Carl chuckled. "Now, I don't know what you're talking about, but it sure seems good to me.

Chapter 3

Road Less Taken

Deborah grabbed the book that was hidden in the hayloft: Mountain Interval by Robert Frost. Exhausted by a restless night's sleep, and just having milked six cows, she settled into the hay and reread her favorite poem:

Two roads diverged in a yellow wood,
And sorry I could not travel both
And be one traveler, long I stood
And looked down one as far as I could
To where it bent in the undergrowth;
Then took the other, as just as fair,
And having perhaps the better claim
Because it was grassy and wanted wear,
Though as for that the passing there
Had worn them really about the same,

And both that morning equally lay
In leaves no step had trodden black.
Oh, I marked the first for another day!
Yet knowing how way leads on to way
I doubted if I should ever come back.
I shall be telling this with a sigh
Somewhere ages and ages hence:
Two roads diverged in a wood, and I,
I took the one less traveled by,
And that has made all the difference.

Deborah hugged the book. Obviously, Frost had been at a crossroads in his life and knew how she felt. Books were like good friends, and why most were banned was a wonder to her. Poetry from Amish papers and books were fine, but Robert Frost just had a way of showing simple life and thoughts through nature.

Her eyes scanned the first line again:

Two roads diverged in a yellow wood

Being autumn, the roads were indeed yellow with oak leaves. And most paths she traveled looked the same at a fork. But after yesterday, she knew she could never marry Noah. The only path left was to move to Smicksburg.

I took the one less traveled by,

And that has made all the difference.

Could it make all the difference in the world, like the poem claimed? Truth be told, she hoped Samuel would return to the Amish, but he left years ago.

Samuel was all she wanted in a man: good looks and good heart. But when it came time for their baptism, he took the vow not meaning it, and asked her to leave too. But not willing to leave, or be engaged to a non-Amish man, he released her, and she'd never found anyone who could match him, or come close. They'd read poetry in this loft together; it was Samuel who introduced her to Robert Frost and she was captivated ever since. Even tried to mimic his style when writing her own poems.

A shadow loomed over her, and she didn't have to look up to know who it was.

"Deborah, what are you reading? Hand it to me."

She obliged him, and braced herself for the fire and brimstone lecture…again. So, she closed her eyes, shooting up a prayer. *Lord, help him see that times are changing…many Amish ways are changing. Amish poems are limited in scope. Lord, help his temper.*

She looked up and the pain in her *daed*'s eyes was unbearable. What a disappointment she was to him. But after a few moments of saying nothing, he collapsed onto the loft floor, appearing to have fainted.

Not knowing whether to leave him or not, she found herself running to the house. Her *mamm* grabbed a bottle of aspirin and other herbs and ran toward the back door. "Go get Dan," she yelled, not looking back.

Dan? Why not go to a real doctor? Dan was an herbalist. *Nee*, her *daed* needed to see the real doc in town. She ran to her horse that wasn't even hitched to the buggy, and led her to a nearby stump, stepped on it, and mounted the horse bareback, and shot toward town.

~*~

Deborah pushed the needle through the cloth, then the batting, making even stitches. She was admired for her even stitching, but truth be told, she didn't like to quilt. The women around the quilting frame were unusually quiet, but not a peace-filled quiet. The strife-filled quiet. And eyes seemed to be on her. Why?

Not one to beat around the bush, she met the gaze of Elizabeth Byler who sat across from her. "So, you've all heard I rode bareback on my horse into town, a few days ago, *jah*?"

The echo of disapproving '*jah*'s' bounced off the walks, scolding Deborah.

"At your age, you should know better," Elizabeth chided.

Not one to talk disrespectfully to an elder woman, she tried to iron out the scowl on her face. "Elizabeth, I know. I panicked."

More silence.

"My *daed* has an irregular heartbeat, the doctor said. Needs to take some new medicines."

Elizabeth groaned. "An English doctor, of all things. Why not Dan?"

"Because Dan isn't a real doctor."

"Herbs cure just as well as those chemicals they put in those new medicines. God made the trees for our healing." Elizabeth made no attempt to smooth her furrowed brow.

"*Jah*," chimed in Emma Sue, her lifelong friend. "You've always trusted the English too much."

Deborah shoved the needles into the blue cotton fabric. "My *daed*'s listening to the English doctor with the blessing of our bishop. My *oma* thanked me for saving his life."

Tsk. Tsk. Tsk. Your *oma*'s too friendly with the English, too. Has them over regularly for tea and coffee."

No one talked about Deborah's *oma* in a negative tone without hearing from her. "My *oma* lives out her Christian faith, being hospitable, opening her door to those in need."

"*Ach*, those neighbors of hers aren't in need," Elizabeth snapped. "They seem rich to me."

"Rich in material things, is all. My *oma* listens and prays with Margaret over tea and cookies. Something we should all be doing."

"Humph. I will not. What fellowship does light have with darkness?"

Deborah knew this verse from the Bible inside and out. But she'd also read to love your neighbor as yourself, the greatest command. Her *oma* was doing the right thing, and Elizabeth was judging another person, being guilty of sin. Were things different in Smicksburg? Did the settlement have an *ordnung* that was a higher order? Higher way of thinking?

"I saw Samuel in town. Has a fancy new car."

Deborah's head spun towards Emma Sue. "So?"

"Well, he's a driver for the Amish now."

A driver? She needed a ride to Smicksburg, but she wouldn't dare ask Samuel. Old feelings had a way of resurrecting themselves.

"Is he charging a reasonable price, or is extortion his game?"

Elizabeth's remark made everyone stop sewing. Emma Sue was the one to speak up. "Elizabeth, that is not kind. Samuel's shunned, but it doesn't mean he isn't leading a *gut* life."

"*Jah*," Deborah couldn't hold it in any longer. "He felt that the *Ordnung* was too strict. He believed God didn't care about the size of the brim on his hat."

"It's a sign of inward rebellion," Elizabeth warned. "We live in unity, *jah*? We all dress the same."

Deborah bit her lip, because what she wanted to say was, *some in our Gmay wear sheep's clothing and are wolves*. As the tea kettle whistled, she knew she needed to leave before she boiled into a heat that would not whistle sweetly.

~*~

Jeb read the letter over again.

Dear Jeb,

I miss you. Won't you consider coming back, repent, and be a part of our fold again? As you know I write to Emma secretly, because I really want to know if our Ordnung is too strict. Well, it seems like the Ordnung in Smicksburg is too lenient. Clothes of different colors show pride. How can you go to church, wearing the same things, but be in different colors? That doesn't show unity. You know black and blue have been our colors for centuries.

Jeb, I fear for your soul. I fear you may end up burning in hell, where there is gnashing of teeth.

Love,

Sarah

Jeb thought of all that Carl said about God looking at the heart, and crumbled up the letter, and threw it in the woodstove. The letter will burn, not me, he grimaced.

He returned to the oak table, raking his fingers through his shaggy blonde hair.

"Looks like you've made up your mind, *jah?*" Emma asked, placing more pancakes before him."

"*Danki*, Emma. And, *jah*, I'll be staying. Seeing things mighty different."

Emma sat across from him, concern filling her green eyes. "Don't be angry."

Jeb cut through the stack of pancakes. "I've been fed a lie for so many years; it's hard not to be. I feel *forhold* in the head."

"So, did Abe at first. Me too. We all lived under such condemnation for so long; it's hard to live without fear…"

"Fear of going to hell?"

"*Jah*," Emma said. "But I'm believing the whole Bible now, and when those feelings come, I say out loud, "For there is therefore no condemnation to those who are in Christ Jesus…"

Jeb lowered his head. "Emma, I don't even know what that means…"

"*Jah*, you do. Abe explained it the other night."

"I know it in my head, but not in my feelings. To accept that God loves me is hard."

Emma poured more coffee into Jeb's mug. "It takes time, just like anything else. But look for it. God's creation is filled with His nature. The nature of God is *wunderbar*."

Jeb scratched his chin. "When Carl and I first came here, we saw a sunset like no other, and I thought of the scripture, 'The heavens declare the glory of God'. Is that what you're talking about?"

"Exactly. When I feed my birds, I think of how not one sparrow falls without God knowing and caring. I struggle too. We both lived under that *Ordnung* back in Cambria County."

Jeb looked across the table at Emma. How he wished he could find a woman who he could talk to as freely as her. One who he could reason with.

"So, now that you're staying, you'll need a job. I hear there's one at the saw mill down the road."

"At the Bylers?"

"*Jah*. Best go today before it's snatched up."

Jeb nodded, and continued to work on the plate of pancakes in front of him.

"Jeb, you'll meet someone you love more than Sarah. At least that's my prayer…"

"I was hoping the letter would have said she was coming out…"

"She's afraid, Jeb. Like we were. I do write her a lot, and you never know. Maybe she will end up here, too."

Jeb had met some girls at church yesterday, but very few his age that weren't married. But he was trying to believe that God cared enough to answer his prayer for a wife. A real helpmate he could walk through life with…someone to love.

Chapter 4

Granny Leaves Millersburg, Ohio

Deborah folded the last of her aprons and neatly placed it in her little green Samsonite suitcase. She'd had this piece of luggage since she was a child, and how she loved to pack it to stay overnight at her *oma*'s. Her *oma*, the woman who was more like a *mamm*, her own *mamm* being so busy raising a large family. Even though she wasn't even married, Deborah longed for the days when she could just sit and knit and be a granny. And for that to happen, she needed a husband.

She heard her driver beep the horn outside, and her heart jumped into her throat. She'd said good-bye to everyone, but her *mamm*, who was down in the kitchen. Bracing herself, she made her way down the long staircase.

Catch me, Daed.

Go, ahead, honey. I'll catch you.

But I'm afraid.

You can trust me. Jump!

It was if her *daed* was saying it out loud, so vivid was the memory. She did jump and he did catch her, over and over again, through the years. Could she trust her Heavenly Father to catch her if she fell in Smicksburg? If she failed to ever find someone to love?

Deborah raced to the kitchen to bid farewell to her *mamm* quick-like, so she wouldn't cry. But her *mamm* held her embrace, and whispered, "Take care, my little Deborah. You're always welcome back home." And she couldn't hold back the tears and wept on her *mamm*'s shoulder.

"We'll see you on Christmas, *jah*?"

"*Jah*, and Old Christmas t-too," she stammered. "Take care of *daed*. Try to get him to take his medicine."

"He has his herbs and will do just fine."

"Please, *Mamm*. You know times are changing. They have those machines now for further testing."

"He'll get an EKG at the hospital. I promise."

"Danki, *Mamm*. Write often." She kissed her cheek and ran out the side door to her driver. But as she neared the car, she heard the oddest song.

My boyfriend's back and you're gonna be in trouble
Hey-la-day-la my boyfriend's back
You see him comin' better cut out on the double
Hey-la-day-la my boyfriend's back

When she opened the door, she gasped. "Samuel? What on earth?"

He turned the radio down. "Sorry, Deb. That song comes on all the time. Ironic though…"

"What?" she sputtered.

"The words to the song…My boyfriend's back. I didn't plan it."

"Samuel, I didn't think you did, but did you plan to drive me on purpose?"

"The driver who was supposed to take you is sick. Called me up to take his spot."

"Well, you know I can't go with you in the car…for three hours. It wouldn't be right." She couldn't help but keep her eyes glued to his chocolate brown eyes…that matched his hair. They were so mellow; they always calmed her down. "I really shouldn't."

"Because I'm shunned?"

"*Nee*. We can ride with shunned Amish, and you know that..."

"Then what is it?"

She couldn't say it out loud, but in her heart, she knew. She was afraid of falling in love with him again. Had she ever really gotten over him? And if he started to talk about why he left, he might try to persuade her to leave too. But then again, didn't the Bible say our faith would be tested with fire? Could she get stronger if she accepted the ride? Maybe see Samuel as he is today, and not as he was, living in the past.

She got into the car. "Now, drive slow. I don't like how cars zoom up and down the street these days."

Samuel chuckled. "*Ach*, you haven't changed much."

"What's that supposed to mean?"

He put the car in reverse and flashed her a smile. "You always spoke your mind, and I'm glad you still do. Some Amish women can't seem to find their voice. It's sad."

"Well, I know what you mean, but it's not for me to judge."

Samuel looked intently on the road. "Lots of rain lately. Flash flood warnings out."

"But it's a clear day."

"Rained real hard north of here, and when we get into Pennsylvania, those windy roads with hills sometimes get real dangerous." He looked over at her. "Put on your seatbelt."

Deborah hardly ever drove in a car with seatbelts. They were somewhat new. She looked over at the strap to her right and brought it across her lap, and took the metal latch and tried to fasten it.

"Having trouble?"

"I can get it."

She fumbled around some more, but to no avail. Samuel pulled into the nearest parking lot and turned to her. "Here, let me do it. They're not called safety belts for nothing." He reached down and covered her hands with his.

She didn't pull away, even though she knew she should. *Lord, forgive me.*

"I've missed you, Deb."

She couldn't lie. "And I've missed you, too."

"Even after all these years, I still think of you." He lowered his head. "I've tried."

"Haven't you met a nice girl yet?"

"*Nee*, and sometimes, I wish I'd never left the Amish."

Deborah squeezed his hands tight. "You can repent and be restored."

"But I have too much of the English modern ways in me. Deb, you don't know what you're missing."

Deborah knew she'd have to turn from him…shun him…if he tried to make her doubt her faith.

"I see how hard the Amish women work, hanging up clothes after scrubbing them on a washboard. Do you know there're ringer washers and clothes driers now? Almost everyone has them. Wouldn't you like to have more free time?"

Deborah stiffened. "I like to hang laundry."

"In the winter?"

"In the winter. Well, unless there's a blizzard," she said in nervous laughter.

Samuel pulled out of the parking lot and drove at a slow, even pace. Deborah saw trees swaying in the wind and the motion of the car made her dizzy, so she looked ahead. Only problem was, she could see Samuel out of her peripheral vision.

"So, why are you moving to Smicksburg? I hear they're more lenient. Higher Order of Amish."

"I suppose so. My Uncle Isaac and Aunt Mary have a saw mill out there and really like it."

"So, you're going to help with their *kinner*?"

"*Nee*. Their *kinner*, my cousins are all grown and married."

Samuel tapped the steering wheel. "Then you've met someone out there and will be wed?"

Deborah knew her heart could flap like the wind right now. If she said she wasn't courting anyone, he'd pursue, she was sure. And she might give in... "*Nee*, I'm not attached to anyone in a marrying way."

The car slowed to the pace of a buggy. "Deb, if the Amish in Smicksburg are more lenient, having an

Ordnung that didn't choke me, I'd be willing to give it a try...for you."

Deborah felt her mouth grow dry. Was he serious? Of course, he was. Samuel never said anything unless he meant it. It was one thing from his Amish heritage he took pride in; his word was as good as his name.

She felt him take her hand. "What do you say, Deb?"

"I, ah...I'm in shock. Didn't expect this, and need lots of time to think."

"So, if I get my old Amish clothes out, make things right with the bishop in the new settlement in Pennsylvania, you'd consider marrying me?"

Of course, I would! She wanted to shout, and throw her arms around him. But she knew better. She could not accept a proposal of marriage from a man not Amish. "Samuel, you seek God and follow the path He has for you. If it's in Smicksburg, and our paths cross, by God's will, then I'd have to say I'd be mighty happy."

~*~

"I have to use a diesel engine?" Jeb gasped. "Not saw by hand?"

Isaac slapped his knee, not able to stop laughing, and once again, Jeb felt out of place. "We sawed by hand in Cambria County."

Isaac sobered abruptly. "*Ach*, then no wonder you're hesitating. You were Swartzentruber?"

"*Jah*. And I'm surprised at how much the Amish have given in to the ways of the world."

"We're not attached to the world in any way. We don't have any bills or payments to attach us."

Jeb shook his head. "If you couldn't buy diesel, you'd be out of business, *jah*?"

Isaac scratched his salt and pepper beard. "No, we know how to saw by hand. It would take us longer, but we'd still be able to do it. And we use water power too. Diesel's kind of new."

"Water's free and comes from the *gut* Lord. Why not just use it all the time?"

"Streams not running all the time. In spring, it's all water power, though, due to the winter thaw." Isaac looked at the clock in his shop. "Do you want the job or not. I need to get back to work."

Jeb felt like he was skating on ice. Not being a good skater, he wobbled a lot. Was it right to use diesel? He'd never even considered it. But he needed to make a living and a man who didn't work was worse than anything. "I'll take the job, for now."

"For now?"

"Until my conscience tells me otherwise. I need a job and I'm thankful you can give me one."

Isaac readjusted his black wool hat, and Jeb noticed the rim wasn't as wide as the ones back home. And it was considered wrong. Condemnation threatened to overtake him, and then he thought of what Carl said. God doesn't care about the color of your clothes. He looks at your heart. This whole process of adjusting to a whole new way of thinking was tiresome…mighty tiresome.

"We're expecting company today," Isaac yelled over the shop to Jeb. "My niece. She's a cutie."

"Aw, how old is she?"

"Twenty-one."

"*Ach*, I thought she was a little girl by your tone. Why isn't she married yet?"

"She turns everyone down, is why. She said yes to one man, but he strayed from the Amish faith and got himself shunned. Had her heartbroken a few years back, and hasn't been able to recover. That's what I've been told." He readjusted his hat again. "She writes my Mary, and says the silliest things. She said the Bible says to trust in no man."

"It does," Jeb said with a grin. "But she's using it out of context."

"Exactly. She needs to find a man that she can trust." He snapped his fingers. "Hey, maybe it's you. I saw the young women at church trying to get your attention. I overheard one go on and on about your eyes. One said they're gray, another, a mixture of blue and gray." He walked up close to Jeb and stared. "They are gray. I'll be."

"They're hazel, like my *mamm*'s were."

"Were? Aren't your folks alive?"

Jeb bit his lower lip, surprised at the emotion that welled up so quickly in him. "My parents were hit by a car, and died, a year ago. So, I left the farm and came to stay with Abe."

Isaac put his hand on Jeb's shoulder. "I'm real sorry. You know you have the support of our *Gmay*, *jah?*"

"*Jah*. I know. I just miss …."

Before Jeb could finish, Isaac snapped his fingers. "I knew it. You're using things you feel are too modern; Abe felt like that for a while too."

"*Jah*. We both agreed the *Ordnung* only dealt with rules and regulations, but nothing about the inner man that the Bible talks about."

"I'm kind of new here too. Came out from Millersburg, like most of the people here. Land's cheap, especially wooded land. After a few months, I felt right at home."

Jeb heard the clopping of horse's hoofs racing down the road. When he turned to see who it was, he felt the blood drain. His brother, Abe had Carl in the buggy; and blood gushed from Carl's head."

Abe jumped out of the buggy when it came to a halt. "Jeb, I'm glad you're still here. We need help."

Jeb ran over to Carl and took his hand. "What happened?"

Though his lower lip was swollen, he managed to say, "Whites…hitchhiking."

Jeb looked at Abe for an answer. He didn't know Carl had left. "He said he'd write you, but said it was too hard to say good-bye in person."

Jeb pulled Carl to him and embraced him. "My brother. Let's get you to the doctor."

Isaac ran into the house to get some rags, and Jeb bowed his head and prayed to a God he was trying to see as loving.

Chapter 5

~~~

Not Love at First Sight

As the sun began to hide behind the mountains, Deborah knew Samuel was nervous. Streams of water covered the roads and he'd already slid a few times. But through the rain drenched windows, she could see the dense woods of Pennsylvania, and was in awe. She'd never been to this state before, and had never seen such windy roads that twisted up and down hills. Although a little nervous, she was eager to see Smicksburg, especially with Samuel with her.

"Almost there, Deb. Only a few more minutes. Can I see the address to your uncle's place again?"

She handed him the map she'd been following the whole trip. Fascinated by maps and other places, it was a wonder she'd never traveled before. Although homesickness threatened her to break down in tears, she kept her chin up. God had a plan…and Samuel might be in it…

"Looks like we're on the right road. What's the house number again?"

"294 Locust Road. We just passed 284. So slow down and look for a saw mill."

"We've passed several. Must be a big industry here. Providing lots of jobs, *jah*?"

She turned to him and smiled. "*Jah* and I hear my uncle is looking for some help."

"There's a saw mill with Byler on the mailbox. This must be it." Samuel pulled into the long dirt road that led to a white farm set behind the saw mill. "Wow, this is a nice place."

"*Jah* sure is. And their curtains are white. I've noticed all the curtains peeking through the Amish farms are white, not light blue. Must be the color here. I like it." When the car came to a stop, she expected her aunt and uncle to come out on the porch, arms wide open. But there was no one to greet them. How odd. There were a few buggies hitched up, but no greeting committee.

She got out of the car and Samuel ran around to canopy her with an umbrella. "*Danki.* I'll go see if I can get some help with my belongings."

Samuel took the small suitcase out of the back seat. "I can handle this," he said with a smile. "Do you mind if I come in and talk to your uncle about a job and the *Ordnung* in his *Gmay*?"

Deborah couldn't hide her hopes. "I'd like that. And you know my uncle and aunt always liked you."

They made their way up the front porch steps, and Deborah opened the front door. But the front room was dark and the only light came from the kitchen in the back. "Uncle Isaac? Aunt Mary?"

She soon saw her uncle race into the living room. "Hi there, Deborah. So *gut* to have you."

"Is something wrong?"

"Well, kind of. Have a visitor in the kitchen that's mighty afraid of being found."

"Why?"

"Come and see."

"Uncle Isaac, Samuel Yoder is with me. He'd like to talk to you about work…and returning to the Amish here in Smicksburg."

"Welcome Samuel. Didn't see your face out here in the dark. You can both come back to the kitchen."

When she entered the kitchen, it wasn't what she expected. No surprise welcome, but a man badly beaten, groaning in a rocker near the stove. A tall man with blond hair was spoon feeding him. "What happened?"

The man who fed the man turned and she looked into his eyes. By the oil lamp light, they were the oddest color; grayish-like. And they were so kind. He stood up and offered her his chair. "I'm Jeb. And this is my friend, Carl. Got beat-up while hitchhiking. Tis a pity."

"*Jah*, for sure. I'm Deborah, Isaac and Mary's niece. And this is Samuel, my driver. We just got in from Ohio."

"How's your horse?" Jeb asked Samuel. "Must be exhausted."

Deborah looked at Jeb, one eyebrow cocked. "We didn't ride a horse from Ohio. Samuel has a car."

Jeb's gray eyes grew stormy. "Amish don't drive in cars."

"Well, Samuel's not Amish..."

Jeb put a hand up in protest. "An Amish woman doesn't accept a ride in a car."

Abe walked over to the woodstove, rubbing his hands together for warmth. "Deborah, I'm Abe, Jeb's brother. I moved here from Cambria County a while back, but Jeb just got here last week. We were raised Swartzentruber, and so even being a passenger in a car is a sin."

Samuel gawked. "I've read about the Swartzentrubers, but never met one. Is it true you don't even plant flowers, thinking it being vain, or proud, or something?"

Jeb nodded. "It is vain."

Deborah was speechless. She'd never met such an opinionated Amish man before. She looked over to her Aunt Mary, who motioned for her to draw closer to her. When she did, she was met with an embrace, and was led into the living room, where she lit a few candles. "Jeb's real upset about Carl. Pay him no mind."

"I should say," Deborah gasped. "Flowers? Is he serious?"

"Well, he was always told it was wrong. His brother and wife just put lattice under their porch. Any decorating was forbidden where they lived."

"And Jeb's wife? Has she gotten far with him?"

Her weary aunt slumped in her chair. "He's single. But not for long. Made a *gut* impression on lots of women last night, at the Singing."

Deborah leaned forward, eager for more information. "He went to a Singing? So, he's not as old as he looks?"

"He's twenty-three."

Deborah covered her mouth, but couldn't silence the hilarity that welled up from within. "He's *twenty-three* and went to a Singing? He is an odd one."

"He's never really sung, having come from the strictest order. He said the hymns were too fast."

Deborah burst into laughter again. "Do you think he'll stay here? I mean, do you think he'll be able to make it, with us higher Order folk?"

Mary sighed. "He only has his brother now. Lost his folks last year in a buggy accident. Mighty hard on him. So, maybe you can help him fit in? He works here."

Deborah did feel sorry that Jeb lost his parents, but if he was abrupt and rude with her again, she'd give him a piece of her mind.

~*~

Later that night, when Jeb and Abe brought Carl back to their place, Jeb stayed up, reading Charles Dickens, and how the Ghost of Christmas Past had come to Scrooge to show him his childhood, locked up in a boarding school. It only made Jeb think of his own childhood, and he was in a similar prison of sorts. So many rules that didn't make sense had made him fail to keep them, and hence, the condemnation he battled.

He thought over his day. How did God show himself to him? The image of his friend bloodied up pierced through his mind, and heart. Where was God? Carl was a believer, so where was the protection the Bible spoke so much of? As soon as he thought this, shame filled him. He should not question God. That too was a sin.

He looked back into the book, and tried to read, but his mind was still on Carl. Was it true that KKK members burnt crosses on property of those who liked Blacks, as a warning? Were they in danger? Were they being watched?

The wind blew the maple tree next to the house and its branches scratched the window near his bed. He had to admit, he was afraid. But an emotion deeper than fear was in his soul too: uprightness. He knew what they were doing to help Carl was right, and it was something engrained in him since a youth. *Upright men shall see His face*; he remembered reading in the Psalms. Was this part of seeing the heart of God today? He had a sense that Carl was brought into his life for a reason, and was God loving and protecting Carl through him?

Peace washed over him, and a deep satisfaction that he was in the right place, for now. God would reveal himself one day at a time, he supposed.

A stone hit his window, or was it the banging of the branches again. No, he was sure it was a pebble, the din louder. What on earth? He blew out the candle on his nightstand, and went to the window. A shadow flashed across the yard. Jeb clenched his fists, and thought of the gun Carl had on him. If those ruffians had come back, could he sit by and watch

Amish Knitting Circle Christmas

them hurt his friend? Lord, I'm a pacifist, but have lived a cloistered life. Help me be faithful to these new temptations. Temptations to strike back.

A loud bang rang from outside, and soon Abe ran down the hall, into his room. "Jeb, we'll trust God, no matter what, *jah*? No fighting back?"

Jeb felt pressure on his face as his blood pressure rose. "I'll not let them hurt Carl."

"You can only stand between them, Jeb. You know that."

To Jeb's shock, loud shouts and laughter were heard from outside. Was it the KKK burning a cross? Abe ran to the window to look outback, then slowly started to chuckle.

"What's so funny?"

"We are. We forgot its Halloween night. Some kids in the neighborhood tipped over our outhouse…and one fell in. Come look."

Jeb tried to make out the image through the dark. Abe was right. The young man's friends had deserted him, leaving him in sewage as they ran off. "Poor fellow," Jeb said. "Looks like he needs some help."

"*Jah*," Abe said. "Let's go dunk him in the fishing hole."

~*~

Deborah sipped her morning coffee, grateful that she'd always been close with her Aunt Mary. If she had to live with her Aunt Sadie, she'd leave after a week. But she already felt at home in a few days. Had Samuel, though? And was she opening her heart up for another disappointment?

"Where are you, Deborah? Back home in Millersburg?" Aunt Mary asked.

"*Nee*. Just thinking…"

"About your *daed* then? I know he needs that test, but he's a stubborn man, just like my Isaac."

"*Daed* will go…I hope."

Aunt Mary got up and poured more coffee into Deborah's blue speckle ware mug. "Spill the beans."

"What?"

"Something's not right. It's not about Samuel, is it? Him wanting to talk to the bishop today…and maybe returns to the People?"

Deborah couldn't hide the hope in her eyes. "I am nervous. What if he doesn't see his need to return? And if the *Ordnung* is too strict?"

"Do you think it's too strict? You'll be under the Order too."

Deborah shifted her weight on the oak bench. "Well, there are new inventions to make life simpler. Some of the English have clothes dryers. Can't even believe it. Hot air blown into a spinning machine. No hanging clothes outside…"

"But you always liked hanging clothes outside…."

"Well, Samuel and I talked a lot when we drove out. The Amish waste time by not being more…modern."

"Deborah. Maybe you shouldn't be talking to Samuel. Jeb's a better influence…"

"*Ach*, he's a stick in the mud. Everything I say and do is wrong."

"Like what?"

Deborah felt her teeth clenching. Few people made her clench her teeth, but Jebediah did. "You told me to take him out a mug of strong coffee the other morning, remember? He'd been up helping that kid who pushed over the outhouse to wash-up…"

"*Jah?*"

She clenched her coffee cup so hard, she was afraid it would crack. "He said that the cup had flowers painted on it and was carnal. How rude!"

Her aunt's eyes bulged. "He uses our cups and plates all the time, and never said a word. Wonder why?"

"I do not know, and do not care. I know he's had it hard with his parents…"

Aunt Mary looked at her with disappointment in her eyes. "You could have lost your own *daed*. I thought you'd have more compassion."

She bowed her head. "And I have a healthy *mamm*, too. I'm sorry."

Aunt Mary got up again and poured a mug full of coffee in a large mug with deer on it. "Go ahead on out and take this to Jeb. He likes deer."

"Aunt Mary. Are you trying to be a matchmaker?"

"*Jah*, I am. Jeb's as *gut* as they come. Samuel could ruin you. Best keep your distance from him until he repents and is welcomed back into the flock. No going on walks at night, hear me? Him sleeping in the hayloft will have to change. And soon."

Deborah's mouth dropped open wide. "How could you think such a thing?"

"What? You staying away from a shunned man until he repents? It's in the *Ordnung* and we're agreeing on that, *jah?*"

Deborah didn't say anything, because doubts plagued her ever since she'd been talking and taking long walks with Samuel. The world was changing; the Amish were stuck in time. She took the coffee cup from her aunt, and went out the side door towards the mill.

The early November wind whipped around her, and she knew she made a mistake to leave in haste, not taking her shawl. Well, she wouldn't be staying long at all. She'd just hand him the coffee and march back to the house.

As she went down the dirt path to the large mill in front of the house, she noticed there was frost and ice thickened on mud puddles. Smicksburg got cold so early. Must be the elevation, being in the foothills of the Alleghenies.

When she saw Jeb, he nodded and turned off the diesel engine and the din of the saw mellowed to silence. Deborah handed him the coffee and he stared at the mug. "*Ach*, it has an eight point on it."

"What's that? And do you think it's wrong?" Deborah prepared herself for battle.

"*Nee*, nothing wrong at all. And an eight point is a deer with eight points on its antlers." He took a sip of coffee. "It's *gut*."

"Aunt Mary made it."

Jeb stared at the mug. "You know, that reminds me. Crossbow season's coming up and fast."

Deborah noticed Jeb's gray eyes turned a more turquois color when animated. Aunt Mary had said he was very devout. Was it his love for God that made them seem to glow? "Cross Season. Is that a religious holiday your People observed where you came from?"

Jeb had a mouth full of coffee in his mouth, and turned to let it spray out. He tried to not chuckle too much, keeping his coffee from spilling.

Deborah took even breaths. She would not let the likes of Jebediah Weaver get to her, so she spun around to go back up the long path, but he caught her by the arm. "I'm real sorry," he said, still chuckling. "Cross-bow season is a hunting time. I use a horizontal bow and arrow, so it's called a cross-bow. Nothing to do with the cross, like the one you're thinking of." He scratched his chin. "Don't people hunt in Ohio?"

Deborah looked up at him, mindful of the nearness between them. His gaze met hers with sincerity and kindness. She was too stunned to speak. "What did you just ask me?"

"Ohio. Don't people hunt over there?"

"*Jah*, with guns. I never knew anyone who still used a bow and arrow."

"Well, I set up traps too. I love to hunt, and the price of hides is high; Abe and I always made a *gut* profit."

Deborah gasped. "What do you mean?"

"We sell all kinds of animal fur to traders in Canada. Mostly coon and fox though."

Deborah was always taught to respect animals. They provided food for the table only. "Do you eat raccoons and foxes?"

"*Ach, nee*. We eat lots of squirrel back home. Well, my *daed* said they ate most anything during the Great Depression."

Deborah still didn't know what to say. All she knew was she never met a mountain man before, and this side of Jeb…she had to admit to herself, was attractive. But not attractive enough to steer her attentions from Samuel.

Feeling her cheeks flush, she spun around to continue on the path, but slid and fell forward, and lay on the icy grass before she knew what happened. But instantly Jeb scooped her into his arms and walked briskly towards the house. For some reason, she felt nauseated…and her head hurt. When Jeb got her to her aunt, she thought she heard him say something about a concussion.

"Well, she can't go to sleep, Jeb." Mary said. "Can you stay with her? I'll go fetch Isaac down at the bottom pasture. He'll know what to do."

"I know what to do." He lifted Deborah's chin, peering into her eyes. "*Gut*, pupils aren't dilated." Taking his hand away from her face, Jeb asked her to walk a straight line across the room, which she did.

"She's fine," Aunt Mary said.

Jeb put a hand up. "She's not out of danger. Other signs of a concussion can show up all day."

"Can you watch her then? For these signs?" Mary asked, wiping perspiration from her brow.

"*Jah*, sure," Jeb said. His turquoise eyes boar intently into hers. "Now, Deborah, you need to stay awake, understand? What do you want to talk about?"

Her head throbbed, but she managed to say, "What's it like to be a mountain man?"

Chapter 6

Granny's leaving the Amish?

Later that night, Deborah saw the light flash on her window and knew Samuel wanted to talk. But her head still throbbed, and she just wanted to stay in the nice crisp sheets. Her aunt's warning to stay away from Samuel had also cut her to the heart. Was she being foolish to not take the advice of someone who loved her and was older…wiser?

The light kept glowing on the window. Well, she may as well go down and tell him what she had to tell him years ago. *We shouldn't be seeing each other alone…*

When she lifted her head off the pillow, a pain shot up her neck. Jeb had said she'd be sore for a while. Jeb. He wasn't as strange as she thought, although odd in his thinking. Too strict. But when he talked about his parents with such love and then sadness, she saw a man who had a heart. Could his rough edges come off? And why on earth did she care?

Despite the pain, she reached for her long robe, and tied her hair up to cover with a *kapp*, but the pain in her neck screamed at every move. Descending the long stairway on tip-toes, she felt her way around the living room and then kitchen to open the side door. With no lantern light, she stumbled and made a noise. Would that wake up her aunt and uncle? She hoped not.

Opening the door, there stood Samuel, as handsome as ever. He took her hand. "Let's take a walk?"

"*Nee*, I can't." Deborah could use the excuse of having a mild concussion today, but needed to be direct. "My aunt feels that we shouldn't be alone together. I'm Amish and you may not be."

Samuel stepped inside, still holding her hand. "Your aunt's as strict as Jeb and Abe."

"Jeb and Abe are fine men. Strict, but upright in their hearts."

Samuel sat on the oak bench by the table. "What's up, Deb. You've changed since last night."

"Like I said, my aunt talked with me. And her being older, she's wiser, *jah*?"

Samuel smirked. "Not always. I know some old folks who are daft."

"But my aunt isn't. And she's been happily married for years. So, I weigh her advice mighty heavy." Not wanting to quarrel, she changed the subject. "How did it go with the bishop today?"

Samuel cracked a few knuckles. "They're strict here too, Deb. And with those Swartzentruber brothers moving here, they could influence everyone to think odd stuff. Things that are superstitious to me."

Deborah's heart sank. Obviously, she needed to cut ties with Samuel again. But why would God allow her to be brought together with him, if it wasn't His will. Surely God wasn't trying to break her heart. She cleared her throat, but it seemed like words didn't come easy lately. She was struck almost dumb when talking to Jeb, and now here with Samuel.

"Leave the Amish…for me." He got up and drew her to himself. "Isn't love stronger than man made rules?" He tilted her chin up and planted a tender kiss on her lips. "I beg you, Deb. We can be Mennonite. They have all the conveniences you deserve, especially electricity."

Deborah felt the kiss linger on her lips. How she cared about this man. They'd known each other since *kinner*, and she'd always trusted him. His character was impeccable. "But, Samuel, I'm baptized into the Amish church. I'd be shunned."

"We'd be shunned together. I'm asking you again. Will you marry me?"

The warmth of his breath, so near her face, and the gentle kiss he put on her cheek, then nose, then lips made her think of nothing else. And she gave in to his love, and wrapped her arms around his neck. "Let me think about it. I do love you."

~*~

Aunt Mary woke with a start when she heard a noise downstairs. Always a light sleeper, she got up to see what it was. She tip-toed down the stairs and to her utter shock, heard Samuel and Deborah's voices…filled with love.

She got closer, and heard Deborah try to tell Samuel that her aunt had advised them not to be alone, but he threw caution aside, mocking a well-known fact. *With age comes wisdom.* And if you want a happy marriage, find out from someone who has one. It was common sense.

To make her presence known, she headed toward the doorway, but spun abruptly on her heels and tiptoed back up the steps. *Samuel and Deborah were kissing?* And she heard quite clearly, *we'd be shunned together.*

Mary climbed into bed, cocooning in the quilt. How could her favorite niece, one who was like a daughter, leave the Amish?

Dear Lord,

You are my hiding place; you shall preserve me from trouble; you shall surround me about with songs of deliverance.

She quoted one of the many passages of scripture she'd memorized. Her niece needed protection from someone who would make her stray. *Lord, show her the right path. Deliver her from evil.*

Her mind quickly turned to Jeb. When Deborah was around him, she seemed to grow in her Amish ways. But when around Samuel, she strayed...

Tomorrow she'd tell the bishop what happened...and ask Samuel to leave, and have Jeb over for dinner.

~*~

Deborah snatched a homemade donut from the plate on the table. Something in her aunt's demeanor told her something was amiss. "Did you get bad news, Aunt?"

"*Nee.* Didn't sleep well."

Her aunt didn't turn from the stove to look at her. She always made eye contact, but all morning, she hadn't made an effort. Did she get a letter from her *mamm*? Is her *daed* okay? Surely her aunt would tell her if she got news.

Aunt Mary turned to scoop scrambled eggs on a platter. "Isaac should be in from milking in a minute or so. Then we can eat." She turned again to her stove and fiddled with donuts frying in her black cast iron pan. "Jeb will take you to the bishop's today. I have a note for you to deliver."

Deborah was too stunned for words, but she blurted, "Aunt Mary. I know how to drive a buggy."

"But you're not used to the windy roads like Jeb is."

"I am too. I've driven around quite a bit."

"You had a head injury…."

"I'm fine. Aunt Mary, what's going on?"

She spun around and her eyes were ablaze. "You tell me."

"Tell you what?"

"What's going on in that head of yours?"

Deborah lowered her gaze. "You heard us last night…"

"*Jah*, I did. I came down hearing voices, and your Uncle Isaac knows too. Most likely why he's late from coming in from the barn. His blood is boiling."

"I love Samuel."

She put a hand-up in protest. "I'm sleep deprived and feel I may say something I regret. Jeb will take you to the bishop's. He'll be here soon."

Ach, I am not a kinner. Why does everyone treat me like one. She sprung up from the table. "I best get ready then." She stomped out of the room, ignoring her aunt's request that she eat breakfast first. She had no appetite once again. It was a big mistake to come to Smicksburg. The Amish are too strict, and the Mennonites were looking mighty fine right now.

~*~

Jeb raised his hand to knock on the door, but it opened before making contact, and Deborah, face as red as beets, swung the door open *briskly*. Why was she blushing? Was she sweet on him? They had spent most of the day together, talking about his mountain experiences, but he didn't mean to imply anything. Especially with Sarah maybe coming out on a secret visit.

Deborah didn't say hello, but brushed past him and mounted into the buggy.

"You know, Deborah. You fell because you're quick on your feet." He pointed to a patch of ice on the driveway. She looked ahead, saying nothing. Jeb stepped up into the buggy. "Have I done something wrong?"

"*Ach,* Jeb. You know what's going on."

Stunned by her abrupt reply and sassy tone, he didn't know what else to do but gawk.

"What are you looking at?"

"You. I've never met a woman who speaks her mind like you do. But I've lived among a stricter Amish sect." He flicked the reins and turned the horse around and led it back out of the driveway.

"I'm sorry, Jeb. You really don't know?"

"I keep to my own business. Have problems of my own…"

"Well, I'm truly sorry then. My aunt treats me like a *kinner*." She raised a white envelope. "It's all in here. My transgression to be read by the bishop."

Jeb had been out coon hunting late at night and had seen Deborah out walking with Samuel, a shunned man, and was mighty happy the bishop was strict enough to deliver some discipline

"Jeb, what do you think of the Mennonites?"

"I don't know any. Like I said, I've been pretty sheltered. Why do you ask?"

She crunched the letter. "I think I'm going to convert."

"Leave the Amish? *Ach*, Deborah. Reconsider. You're baptized and made a vow. You made a pledge…"

"But I'm starting to see the Amish are backwards. Why on earth do we live without some modern conveniences?"

"Well, I find the Amish here modern compared to where I come from."

"How so?"

"Diesel engines for one. The noise drowns out nature and wears on my nerves. I like to hear noises the *Gut* Lord created, don't you?"

"But times are changing. Cars can get us places faster. Buggies are a waste of time. Isn't our time important to God, too?"

"I've never ridden in a car, but it looks mighty scary. But think of this. You may get places faster, but look what you're missing."

"Huh?"

Jeb knew Deborah was one hard nut to crack, so he said a silent prayer before answering. "In a buggy, you go slower. You see more of God's creation all around you."

"And catch you a death of cold in winter."

"Fresh air is *gut* for you. My sister had tuberculosis years back, and the doc said she needed to sleep outside, and in winter, keep the windows open."

"Really? Did she get better?"

"*Jah*. She did. Fit as a fiddle with lots of *kinner*. So, I say, stay as close to nature as much as possible."

"What about clothes driers? It's women who hang the clothes outside, take them down frozen, and let – "

"Deborah, don't keep beating around the bush. You want to leave for Samuel."

She nodded her head and fidgeted with the envelope. "How'd you know? My aunt tell you?"

"*Nee*. I see the way you look at each other." He cleared his throat, surprised that what he just said left a bitter taste in his mouth. *Why? Why should he care?*

"When I'm with Samuel, I can think of nothing else. Not even the consequences of a shunning. Isn't that what love is? Willing to give up everything for the one you love? Having a single eye only toward Samuel?"

Jeb slowed the horse. "I'd say it wasn't love for Samuel to ask you to give up so much. I'd call it selfish. Why doesn't he just repent and come back to the Amish for *you*?"

"He knows they're backwards."

"And you agree?"

Again, she was silent, but continued to crinkle up the letter in her hand. Jeb hoped the bishop could read it after she was done with it.

"Selfish? Really?"

"*Jah*. I had a girlfriend back home, and I didn't pressure her to leave the strict *Ordnung* for me. She has parents to look after. And if you convert to another sect while *Swartzentruber*, you're shunned. I couldn't ask her to do that."

"Then you don't love her."

"*Jah*, I wanted to marry her. I figured she'd leave for me, but she didn't."

"I'm sorry, Jeb. Truly, I am. When you're in love, it's all consuming."

"I love God more."

"Huh?"

"*'Thou shalt have no other gods before me.'* The Ten Commandments are clear."

"Huh? What's that have to do with anything?"

Jeb wished the bishop didn't live three miles away. This conversation was draining him. "If I put Sarah before the Lord, then she's an idol."

"*Ach*, Jeb. That's *furhoodled*. How about, 'It's not good for man to be alone'? You're a man in love, and didn't God create love?" She clenched the letter into a ball. "I'm glad you're away from those *Swartzentrubers*."

Jeb sighed. "I might be going back…"

"*Ach*, why? For Sarah?"

"*Nee*. I find the ways of this settlement carnal."

Deborah snickered. "My, my. We've come from two different worlds and we're both Amish. I think the settlement is too strict."

"Well, the Bible says to seek peace. *'If it be possible, as much as lieth in you, live peaceably with all men'*."

Deborah's head spun toward him. "Do you have the whole Bible memorized?"

"Only Ephesians so far. Working on Romans. But I don't mean to brag."

"I have a hard time remembering any scriptures by heart."

"How much time do you put into it?"

Silence again, only the sound of paper being crumbled. "Not much time at all." Again, she looked over at Jeb. "Can the scriptures really help you that much when making a big decision?"

"I wouldn't make a big decision without letting God speak to me through his Word. And get advice from people who know and love me."

"But you left your settlement. Surely your bishop didn't agree."

Jeb cleared his throat. "Truth be told, many of the sect are having doubts about the *Ordnung*. My parents were ready to leave…before they were killed. All my siblings were in on the talks. When my parents went to Glory, they all left, except me. Then my conscience wouldn't allow."

"What happened?"

"My parents' death was hard to accept." As hard as he tried, tears stung in his eyes. "But I wasn't allowed to talk about them, because everyone knew they were given a warning, and were ready to leave." He grabbed at his quivering chin, hoping Deborah wouldn't notice his grief. "When Abe moved here, and I told him of my struggles to stay in a community that looked down on my parents, he was appalled. He advised me to leave, and I took his counsel."

Deborah put her hand on his back. "I'm so sorry. Did they make sure you had visitors every Saturday, according to our way of grieving?"

"*Nee.* No one came over. And when it's you in a big house full of *gut* memories, it can drive you mad." Jeb clicked his tongue and flicked the reins. "Best be getting to the bishop's." Jeb heard a whimper and looked over at Deborah. "What's wrong?"

"*Ach*, Jeb. I feel so sorry for you. And when I met you, I thought you were mean, but you were grieving. I'm so sorry."

Jeb hadn't seen such an emotional Amish woman in his life…but he had to admit, it was attractive. To have a real conversation with his spouse, like Abe and Emma had, was in his prayers. But most likely, Deborah would be leaving with Samuel…

Chapter 7

Change of Heart?

A few days later, Aunt Mary beamed as she had breakfast with Deborah. "That's a wise decision."

Deborah knew the shock of her leaving with Samuel would be too hard to her loved ones to take, so they had several weeks to lessen the blow. Having told Samuel how much she loved him, she said she needed time to make such a big decision. But she'd make it on Christmas, as a surprise to him. He was perfect in every way....

"So, you're seeing the side of Jeb we know?"

Deborah dipped an oatmeal cookie into her coffee. "He's a *wunderbar* man, and he'll make some woman a *gut* husband someday."

"Sure is the talk of the grapevine. Still going to the Singings, and surrounded by hopeful girls. It's those grayish eyes of his, don't you think?

"They're turquoise on the outer rim."

Aunt Mary snickered. "You're taken with him, aren't you, having studied his eyes?"

"Aunt Mary! I am not. I'm a knitter and notice colors, is all." Her aunt pursed her lips, as if trying to scrunch a smile. "I admire Jeb's dedication to the Bible. I'm trying to memorize some passages, but am always tempted to read poetry, and get side tracked."

Aunt Mary took the coffee pot and replenished her cup. "I can help you. When you memorize scripture, it goes from your head into your heart."

"How can you help me?"

"By asking you to recite passages back to me."

"Where do I start though?"

"Well, not Leviticus or Numbers. What's your favorite book?"

Deborah had to admit, she hadn't read it enough to have a favorite. "I like the story of Ruth. It's so romantic."

"How about a New Testament book?" She snapped her fingers. "I know. How about 1 Corinthians 13. It's all about what love is."

Deborah needed to learn how to be a good wife, so learning about love seemed an appropriate step. "When do we start?"

"Well, how about you go read it over several times. Then start at the top and circle all the bigger words. I used to get all caught up on little words and got discouraged."

The side door opened, letting in a gusty wind. Uncle Isaac walked in, head down.

"What's wrong?" Aunt Mary asked.

"I need workers that are going to stay in this settlement. How can I run a business with men that are only trying it out for size?"

"What are you talking about?"

"*Ach*. Jeb told me the girl he courted in Cambria is coming to visit. Most likely to talk him into going back home."

Deborah felt her mouth grow dry, so she took a sip of coffee before speaking. "She's coming here? In a buggy when it's so cold?"

"*Jah.*"

"Well, he won't go back," Deborah blurted. "He can't."

Aunt Mary grinned. "How would you know?

"Because he has no family back there, and doesn't agree with their *Ordnung*."

Uncle Isaac sat next to his wife and poured himself a cup of coffee. "Let's hope he has more sense than Samson. Changing his whole life over one woman."

Deborah moaned. "I'm sure Sarah's not like Delilah."

"We'll soon find out. She'll be here for Thanksgiving. And I want to keep an eye on them, so I invited Abe, Emma and Jeb over for Thanksgiving dinner." He turned to his wife. "If that's okay with you."

"Well, it will make the house seem less empty. Our kids can't make it home."

Deborah got up to clear the table. She hand cranked water into a large pan to heat up so she could wash the dishes. Looking out the window at the many birdfeeders Uncle Isaac kept replenished, she spied a junco, the little gray and white birds that flew in by the droves to her feeder back in Ohio. Homesickness washed over her by surprise. Was her *mamm* making her cherry pies with all the filling she'd helped put up? Selling pies with her *mamm* at the farmer's market was something they both cherished.

Her mind turned to Jeb. Having lost a *mamm* and *daed*, and having no community to help him, would be unbearable. Surely, he wouldn't go back to his old farm...would he? And why did she care?

~*~

Jeb snatched up a new book that Abe had on the shelf. "Who's Robert Frost?"

Emma looked up from her embroidery hoop. "A poet. Talks a lot about nature, and Abe really likes him."

Jeb flipped through the pages and then put it back on the shelf, and reached for his Bible

"Jeb, it's alright to read something besides the Bible."

Jeb scratched his forehead. "You really think so?"

"*Jah*, I'm sure."

"How can you be sure?"

Emma laid down her embroidery. "I've had to think through the *ordnung* we grew up with. When I found out that the term, *'wolves in sheep's clothing'* was taken from Aesop's Fables, that told me Jesus might have read them, or listened to them."

"Come again?"

"You know. When Jesus said some Christians would be wolves in sheep's clothing, well Aesop lived three-hundred-years before Jesus, and Jesus used that fable to teach a lesson."

"Who's Aesop? And should you be listening to fables?"

"Fables are parables."

Jeb couldn't believe everyday was a new discovery for him. And he was being set free. "*Danki*, Emma."

"You're like moldable clay. Think Sarah will be the same?"

"I don't know. We'll find out next week. She'll only be here a few days, so don't expect her to change completely."

Jeb nodded, and took up his pipe and reached for *In the Clearing*, by Robert Frost. He scanned through the table of contents and picked "Blueberries".

You ought to have seen what I saw on my way
To the village, through Morten sons pasture to-day:
Blueberries as big as the end of your thumb,
Real sky-blue, and heavy, and ready to drum
In the cavernous pail of the first one to come!
And all ripe together, not some of them green
And some of them ripe! You ought to have seen!"

Jeb could read no further. Memories of his *mamm* quickly flooded his mind. Long strolls through the woods to get wild blueberries…the sound of blueberries hitting the bottom of the metal bucket…the scent of blueberry pies she'd always make. And how his *daed*'s gray eyes twinkled with delight, looking lovingly over at his wife.

A sob escaped, and he shut the book.

"Jeb, are you alright?" Emma asked.

But he didn't know what to say. Maybe poetry made a person too emotional. "I think I'll turn in for the night…"

He took the book upstairs with him.

~*~

After an hour of knitting a flashy red scarf for Samuel's Christmas present, Deborah settled down into her comfy warm bed. She reached for one of the many books she brought, but felt an unusual pull to read the Bible. 1 Corinthians 13, to be exact. She'd do as her aunt asked, and start with scripture about love. Did her aunt overhear her talk with Samuel before he left? Surely not.

She flipped the pages, having a hard time finding the book. She found Chronicles, but she was pretty sure her aunt said it was a New Testament book. She turned to the table of contents and quickly found the book. She read 1 Corinthians 13 several times, like her aunt suggested, but read verses 4-7 she again:

Love is patient and kind; love does not envy; love does not parade itself, is not puffed up; does not behave rudely, does not seek its own, is not provoked, thinks no evil; does not rejoice in iniquity, but rejoices in the truth; bears all things, believes all things, hopes all things, endures all things.

The beauty in these verses awed her. It was like poetry, even better than Robert Frost. But what was the secret meaning. Poetry always had a hidden meaning.

Love is patient and kind... Who wouldn't be patient with Samuel? He was perfect. And she tried her hardest to be kind when they disagreed. But when she'd refused to leave the Amish before, she had to admit, Samuel was not kind indeed. The more she thought about it, he was mighty impatient with her. During the ride out, he talked about modern conveniences with a passion, but when she gave some of the advantages of a slower life, he talked to her like a *kinner*, impatience revealed through his even tone and measured words. When she continued to debate, he'd raise his hand and say, rather *impatiently*, that she just didn't know any better.

She reread these two verses and felt ill. *Love does not seek its own.* How many times had she resisted the kisses that got downright lustful? Her cheeks burned red when she thought of the time, up in the hayloft, when she let her hair down. Something only her husband should see, but Samuel untied her *kapp* strings, and before she knew if, he'd unpinned her hair and was raking his fingers through it. If Uncle

Isaac hadn't come into the barn, who knows what else she would have let him unpin? And the hard truth to swallow, was that an Amish man who had morals wouldn't be unpinning anything on his girlfriend.

If the Bible was true, did Samuel love her?

~*~

Shaken by last night's breakdown, a letter from Carl was a welcome reprieve from grief that seemed to be harder as the seasons changed…and Thanksgiving was coming mighty close.

Hey Jeb,

What's up? Haven't heard from you in a coon's age. How's life up there in the sticks of Smicksburg?

Hey, man, how are ya? I've been hitchhiking all over the country. That little incident in Smicksburg didn't scare me none. I keep going on…

Pray for this country though. The clashes between the blacks and whites are getting mighty bad. King's been arrested before, and after his 'I have a Dream speech, I fear something's going to give. Like Kings' going to get shot. Lynching is on the up down south.

Jeb, I don't get it. How come people look at a person's skin and judge a man's insides? Never will understand it.

I thought about what you said about being a preacher. I just might. If I can change people's thinkin' by God's Word, I can't think of a better job. And now that I'm twenty-three, I need to think of my future.

How's life on your end? Did you find any pretty girl to take out for a spin on your buggy? Just kidding. Buggies don't spin. I met someone. Man, she's way cool.

Write soon. Don't forget your main man,
Carl.

Jeb shook his head. Why did Carl use '*man*' so much? He reread the short letter again, and wondered if things were really that bad …the King could be shot. He would pray, for sure and for certain.

Abe came in from the side door, rubbing his hands together. "Ready?"

"*Jah*, in a few minutes."

"The turkeys are running now. Hurry up." He blew into his hands. "If we get a turkey, we'll be taking it over to Isaac and Mary's."

"Why?"

"Because they asked us to spend Thanksgiving with them."

"But Sarah will be here."

"And…"

"She may feel uncomfortable. Remember how shocked I was at the Amish here. Deborah will scare her away forever."

"Is that a bad thing?" Abe sat on the bench across the table from Jeb. "Hate to say this, Jeb, but Sarah's…boring. You need someone like my Emma. A woman who you can really talk to. A woman who has an opinion. I mean, you don't want to be married to someone who always agrees with you, because iron sharpens iron, and that's what Emma does for me. Knocks off the rough edges, and I appreciate it."

Jeb leaned on one elbow. "Well, Sarah speaks her mind loud enough when she's not in agreement with me…What brought all this emotion on? You've never spoken so much, and so fast."

Abe grinned from ear to ear. "Emma's pregnant!"

Jeb beamed. "That's *wunderbar*. When's the baby due?"

"In the spring. April. She didn't want to tell me until she was over the first three months. Having so many miscarriages right after finding out she was pregnant, she didn't want to get my hopes up. So, she shouldered the worry by herself. She doesn't have a selfish bone in her body, *jah?*"

Jeb chugged down the rest of his coffee. "Were you serious about Sarah? About her being too agreeable? Or are you more emotional or something?"

"*Nee*, I'm serious. I think you need someone with a backbone...like Deborah."

Jeb rolled his eyes. "I don't think so...."

Chapter 8

Staying Amish!

Deborah went into the living room with her knitting loom, admiring the shades of red as Samuel's scarf progressed, and sat across from her aunt. "What's wrong?"

"I got a letter from your folks."

"Is *daed* alright?"

"*Jah*, he's fine." Aunt Mary leaned her head back in the Amish rocker, eyes closed, lips moving.

"Aunt Mary, you're scaring me. What are you doing?"

"Praying for strength."

"Is someone else hurt?"

Aunt Mary looked down at the letter she held. "I'd let you read this, but it would be too much of a shock, and there's other personal things between your *mamm* and me, so I'll just tell you what it says." She took a handkerchief from her pocket and started to cough uncontrollably. When the coughing spell passed, she reached for the glass of water on the coffee table, and took a sip.

"Deborah, forgive me, but I've been in close contact with your *mamm*. She knows all about Samuel and you, and you wanting to someday wed. But there are things about him you should know."

Deborah kept her nose in her knitting. "Such as?"

"He was engaged and the girl broke it off, for one. And this didn't happen long ago. Mid-summer."

Deborah froze, red yarn held up in one hand. "Who was she and how come I never heard about it?"

"You had no communication, *jah*? He's a shunned man?"

"But the Amish grapevine sends along messages about shunned people too."

"Well, seems like they kept it a secret, her not being Mennonite, but Jewish."

"*Ach...*"

"Her parents objected, and she broke it off." Aunt Mary took a deep breath. "And he lied to you. There was no sick driver; he asked to take you here in hopes of winning back your heart, and try to persuade you to leave the Amish...again."

Deborah covered her face with her hands, trying to hold back her anger. She'd never known Samuel to be deceitful. "Aunt Mary, I've known Samuel since we were *kinner*. He's never deceived me."

"He may have without you knowing it. He says he's Mennonite, because his parents crossed over, but it doesn't mean like he acts like one. He may be as worldly as they come deep inside. Look at how disrespectful he was towards Amish ways."

Deborah couldn't listen to this anymore. Something wasn't right. She knew Samuel and she had his phone number. "I'm going to call and hear this from his own lips. I'm having a hard time believing this *story*."

"Story? Do you think I've made this up?"

Deborah didn't reply, but threw her knitting down on the floor and ran from the room...to the phone shanty.

~*~

Jeb stuck the newspaper under his arm, and pulled into the sawmill. Jumping out of the buggy, he ran to the side door, and banged.

Aunt Mary opened the door. "Jeb. What's wrong?"

"Where's Isaac?"

"In the living room. Come in."

Jeb followed Mary into the living room, expecting to see Deborah too, but she was nowhere to be seen. Feeling sick, he collapsed in a rocker. He handed the paper to Isaac. "Can you believe it?"

Mary went and sat by her husband, eyeing the headlines. "Kennedy slain? By a sniper in Dallas? Oh, dear Lord."

"What's this world coming to?" Isaac barked, turning to hug Mary, as she began to weep. "Where's Deborah?"

Mary only cried louder when Deborah's name was mentioned. Maybe they did treat her like a *kinner*, as Debora said. Surely, she was strong enough to hear this horrible news. "I'll fetch her. Where is she?"

Through sobs, Mary said she was out in the phone shanty. Had been there a while. Amish using a phone at all was hard for Jeb to grasp, but the Smicksburg settlement allowed them in case of an emergency. Was she alright? "I'll go get her."

Jeb dashed from the room, and running through the dimly lit kitchen, almost ran Deborah over. "Are you alright?"

Tears fell down her cheeks. Jeb led her to the bench and turned the oil lantern up to brighten the room. "So, you heard the bad news, *jah?*"

Deborah's eyes grew round as buttons. "My aunt told you?"

"*Nee*, I came here to tell them?"

Tears continued to stream down Deborah's cheeks, so Jeb handed her his handkerchief. "Well, if you don't know, I don't think it's a *gut* time to tell you. Can I make you some hot chocolate? Cup of coffee?"

She buried her face in his handkerchief and wailed.

Jeb ran to sit on the bench next to her. "What is it? Is your *daed* okay?"

She slowly looked up at him. "*Jah*, Jeb. So thoughtful of you to ask…remembering that my *daed* is ill."

He rubbed her back. "We're *gut* friends now, *jah*? And I care about you."

Deborah stopped trembling and she slowly got up. "I should be asking you if you want coffee. Do you?"

"*Nee*, it's late. But can never pass up a cup of hot chocolate…if you're up to it."

"I am." She poured the glass bottle of milk into a pan, and placed another small log into the cook stove. "What news do you bring?"

"Well, I wish it wasn't such bad news, but it is. The President's been shot."

"Oh, my. That's horrible. And he has a wife and *kinner*." Once again, tears sprang from her eyes and covered her face with Jeb's hanky.

"Wish you weren't already upset to hear such shocking news."

"I'll be fine. What's happened to me is nothing compared to this news."

"But you were sobbing. Come on. You can talk to me."

Deborah turned to check the temperature of the milk. "Well, one Bible verse I'll have in my heart forever. *Trust no man.*"

Jeb tapped the table with his long fingers. "Well, it says not to trust in chariots and horses, but to trust in God." Feeling like he was in uncharted waters, never sharing anything so personal with a woman outside his family, he wished he hadn't pushed for an answer. "Samuel, you're talking about?"

She nodded. "He deceived me in a horrible way. And I feel like such a fool. Blabbing on and on to everyone about how much I loved him, and he me…I was deceived." She turned to pour hot milk into a mug, added cocoa and sugar and set it before Jeb.

"Danki, but there's flowers on the mug…"

She looked at him searchingly, and when she realized he was joking, she smiled. "You've come a long way over these past several weeks. Now you're joking. That's *gut.*"

"*Ach*, I've joked before, but you didn't notice." He took a sip of the hot liquid. "I shot a nice turkey today. And we trapped several foxes and a coon."

She sat across from him. "Jeb, the mountain man."

"*Jah*, that's me. And I was going to bring the turkey over for Thanksgiving next Thursday, but we should fast."

"Fast? On Thanksgiving?"

"*Jah*, to mourn the loss of our president."

"It's Friday, so most likely we'll fast on Sunday." She tilted her head. "Would your people back home fast on a day to celebrate?"

"I think this news has me *furhoodled*. Of course, we can celebrate, and I'll bring the turkey and you can meet Sarah."

"She's coming here? To stay?"

"We'll see. It's in God's hands. Like I said before, I won't be putting her before God and my conscience."

Deborah's eyes caught him off guard. Such light blue eyes seemed to be admiring him. "I wish I was as wise as you. Like I said, I was a fool. Almost leaving the Amish over…Oh, I can be so impulsive."

Jeb had to admit, since Deborah started to share her weaknesses, not being a know-it-all, he found her mighty attractive. Attractive indeed.

~*~

On Thanksgiving Day, Jeb was as uncomfortable as when he used to wear wool underwear. Every nerve seemed to scream out for help. Sarah had arrived, as planned, but he felt nothing. Actually, everything she did bothered him. The constant undertone in her voice was degrading, although she wouldn't say what was on her mind.

Unlike Deborah. Over the past week, she'd shared more about herself. Her ambition to not only have a large family, but to have a husband she could respect really melted his heart. He thought Deborah was headstrong at first, but then again, he was pushing his old ways on her. Since then, he'd taken a ride in a car, and found it convenient for sure. No one knew, but his driver wanted to stop in at his folk's house to watch the president's funeral on television. Since lots of folks didn't have a TV yet, there were thirty-some people watching, sobbing, sharing the pain they experienced.

If I told Deborah I watched a television she'd laugh to no end. He groaned and looked down at the letter in his hands. Why was he always thinking of Deborah!

By the handwriting, he could tell it was Carl. He'd gotten it yesterday, but with Sarah arriving, he'd put off reading it.

Hey Jeb,

Guess you've heard the bad news. Man, can you believe it? And I think I know why he was shot. He was for civil rights. His brother, Bobby was real outspoken about it, and people were afraid the president was on our side. Seems like the world gone crazy. Come Lord Jesus.

Well, I decided to be a preacher-boy. Mama always said I'd be a good one, and I'm taking her advice, and yours. You know Jeb, I never met a white man as nice as you. Wish other men would grow up and act like you.

I'll be hitchhiking up North again. I'm steering clear of the south. What are you doing for Christmas? Can't think of anyone I'd rather spend the holidays with than you groovy folks up there in Smicksburg.

I know I'm hip, and you're a square as they come, but we can hang out. Just don't go telling anyone that Cool Carl digs Amish-folk.

Take care man,
Carl.

Jeb was elated to be able to spend Christmas with Carl. Missing his parents most around this holiday, Carl would be a real distraction. He took a puff on his pipe, and went out into the kitchen where Emma and Sarah were making the turkey and lots of pies.

"*Gut* news, Emma. Can you guess who that letter was from?"

"*Jah*, I can tell by the handwriting."

Sarah rolled pie dough out on the counter. "Who are you talking about?"

"My friend, Carl. I picked him up when coming here."

Sarah slowly looked up at him, eyes narrowed. "Was he Amish?"

"*Nee*, just someone in need." He turned to Emma. "He's coming here to spend Christmas. *Ach*, I'm so glad."

"*Jah*," Emma said smiling. "Will take your and Abe's mind off your parents."

Sarah's mouth parted. "An Englisher will be staying in this house?"

Jeb knew how shocked he was at first when he arrived at Smicksburg. "The folks here take love real serious. It's a greater command than any law."

"Higher than the *Ordnung*?" she hissed.

"The *Ordnung* should be based on it. God is love, not fear."

Emma put up two hands. "Please. Let's not argue today…like yesterday." She put a hand over her expanding middle.

Jeb nodded. "Sorry Emma. In your condition, you don't even have to house me for all the trouble I bring."

"*Ach*, Jeb. I love having you here. What did Carl say about the president being killed? His people have suffered so much, and I hear Kennedy wanted to help them."

"His people?" Sarah shook her head in confusion. "What's that mean?"

Jeb felt the hairs on the back of his neck start to stick out. "He's black."

"What? You mean he's…not white?"

"*Jah*, he's not. And I know your folks are prejudiced and all, but it's just not right. We're equal in God's eyes, so should we be aiming to think like that?"

Sarah slowly put the rolling pin down, dusted off her apron and left the room.

Annoyed, Jeb followed her. "Sarah, I think Emma needs help, being pregnant and all."

"I'm getting my brother and we're leaving. Today."

"He's not here."

She went to the side window. "His buggy's here, so of course he is."

Jeb sat down on a rocker, inhaling the pipe smoke evenly to calm his nerves. "He went with Abe to Indiana. It's only fifteen miles from here."

She cocked an eyebrow. "How did they get there?"

"In a car. In a brand, new 1963 Pontiac to be precise. And he wants to stay here!" Jeb knew he shouldn't have blurted out in anger, but she'd pushed him around for the past two days, and he'd had enough.

Sarah ran up the stairs crying...Jeb went back to his chair to read Robert Frost.

Chapter 9

Thanksgiving

Deborah thought of her family back home in Ohio, it being a holiday. She always liked the fact that her family celebrated Thanksgiving, something not all Amish understood. But they always got together and had a grand feast.

As she rolled out more pie crusts, she wondered if she needed to take advice from people around her, like Jeb said. Like her Aunt Mary had said. Noah was her *daed*'s choice for her. Had she stepped outside God's will, the protection he gave and the burdens he lifted, by coming to Smicksburg? The pain caused by Samuel's deception made her leery of all men, but Noah, she could trust him. He'd never deceived her.

The more she thought about the farm he bought, saying she could have sheep to have wool to spin, was maybe his way of saying he loved her; that was something that he was never able to do. And the buggy ride incident. *Ach*, he cared for his horse as much as a family member and he was most likely checking to see if she was injured.

Deborah poured the pumpkin pie filling into the crust, and slid it into the oven. Out of the corner of her eye, she saw a black buggy go past the window. "Aunt Mary, they're here. Can I go upstairs and freshen up a little bit?"

"*Jah*, sure. You've been such a help." Her aunt embraced as she passed. "Are you alright? I did the right thing, *jah*?"

"*Jah*, you did. Samuel admitted the truth; he was on a rebound and apologized. But my guard is up now. I don't think I'll trust too many men ever again."

Her aunt's countenance dropped. "Don't go down that slippery slope. When you love others, you think the best, believe in them...remember 1 Corinthians 13?"

Deborah didn't even attempt to hide her grief. "Maybe it's Samuel and the president shot on the same day that made it all too much. I think I need to go home."

"We'll talk after dinner. Don't make a big decision when you're hurt."

Deborah heard voices outside and ran out of the room, not wanting Jeb to see her covered in flour. *Why should she care?* But her *oma* said reactions tell the truth, not actions so much. She held her middle, feeling it flip. No, she would not fall for Jebediah Weaver, as fond as she'd become of him over the past few weeks. No, she'd guard her heart; it was in the Bible to do so.

She ran upstairs and peeked through her bedroom to see if she could get a glimpse of Jeb's girlfriend. When Jeb looked up at her window, she quickly put back the white curtain into place. But she could see enough through the cloth to see he was gone, so she put back the curtain again. There stood a beautiful woman, auburn hair peeking through her black bonnet. A cute little turned up nose, high cheekbones and full lips. Even though her black dress came the whole way down to her feet, it looked attractive on her slim figure.

Again. Why did she care? She wished Jeb happiness; he deserved a good wife…because he was a *wunderbar* man. But not to be trusted for sure and for certain…

~*~

Aunt Mary greeted her guest with warm embraces, and Jeb tried his best to not take Sarah aside when she very coolly addressed Mary. Her brother, Jacob, on the other hand, was as friendly as ever. That Jacob wasn't married was a mystery. At twenty-four, he just hadn't found the right girl. But his good looks had women flock to him like geese to calm water.

Would Deborah fall for him? He put his hand to his head, shocked at the thought. Surprised that right now, he'd have to admit he'd be jealous if she did show Jacob more attention than him. He'd seen her looking out her bedroom window; she was staring at Jacob. Did she prefer men with dark hair? Brown hair and brown eyes?

Mary asked them to have a seat at the long oak table, and once again, Jeb gawked at Sarah. She made no attempt to help in the kitchen, which was the

Amish way. The women cooked and the men sat and waited. She'd said she came to see what other settlements were like outside the Swartzentrubers. It was obvious she'd made up her mind and she deemed herself superior. *How arrogant.*

Deborah appeared in a new mauve dress and white apron. She looked beautiful. "Happy Thanksgiving, Deborah," he said, his eyes glued to hers.

"*Danki*, Jeb." She nodded to Sarah and Jacob. "So, your Jeb's friends from Cambria County? Welcome."

Sarah gripped the side of the table and slightly nodded her head.

Jacob's eyes lit up. "Nice to meet you. I'm Jacob and this is my younger sister, Sarah. We understand you're new to Smicksburg, too."

"*Jah.* I came at the end of September."

"And how do you like it?" Jacob prodded.

Deborah sighed. "Well, today, I'm homesick, it being Thanksgiving."

"What does that have to do with it?" Sarah said snidely.

Deborah's light blue eyes seemed to get a tad darker. "It's a holiday. This is my first holiday away from home."

"We don't celebrate Thanksgiving back home," Sarah shot back. "It's not a Christian holiday."

Deborah looked at Jeb, stumped.

"Now, Sarah, we've told you every settlement is different."

Her head spun around and she glared at Jeb. "Pink? *Ach*, it's carnal."

"What?" Jacob asked, his cheeks turning red.

"I knew there were some minor differences, but only the Mennonites wear colors. We wear black and blue to not show pride."

Deborah leaned closer to Sarah. "How about being rude? Is that something that is okay back in Cambria County, too?"

Jacob sprang to his feet. "I'm sorry. She's in shock and doesn't mean to be…rude."

Deborah nodded, and looked over at Sarah. "I remember when I first met Jeb. He was nervous and thought us carnal too. But we talked about what's really important." She covered her heart. "Christ in here, *jah*? And serving him from the heart?"

Sarah would not make eye contact with Deborah, but Jeb couldn't take his eyes off her. She'd been reading scripture and grown in her faith. And since Samuel left, she seemed settled. She would not be leaving the Amish for Samuel. And for that he was glad.

Jacob watched Deborah go to the stove to check the turkey. He turned to Jeb and winked. Jeb shrugged his shoulders, not understanding his meaning. Jacob slid down the bench and whispered in Jeb's ear. "Deborah's a peach. Is she courting anyone?"

"*Nee*. Just got over a break-up."

A smile slid across Jacob's face. "Does she go to Singings?"

"*Nee*. Thinks she's too old. But I go."

"I'm going to ask her to go. Maybe I came to Smicksburg for a reason; maybe I've found the one that's for me."

Jeb got up and briskly walked toward the side door. "Where are you going?" Jacob asked.

"Bring in more firewood."

"We have plenty, Jeb," Deborah chimed in.

"Well, I'll go split more then."

~*~

When everyone had eaten and all the pumpkin pie devoured, Deborah felt like she could barely lift the pan she needed to wash. That Sarah didn't help baffled her Aunt Mary and herself. Even Emma helped, and she was pregnant.

"What's wrong with her?" Deborah asked in hushed tones to Emma.

"She's really a dear friend to me, but this visit hasn't gone well."

"How so?"

"She's trying hard to get Jeb to see he needs to go back to Cambria County. All she's done is point out the differences between Cambria and Smicksburg since she got here, and she made Jeb's nerves raw."

Deborah looked out into the living room where Sarah sat next to Jeb. "Will he leave then? Go back home?"

Emma scrubbed the pot with increased vigor. "Not really sure. They talk a lot in private, but Sarah wanted to go home today, but her brother is staying. So, she's having a hard time. May lose Jeb and a brother she adores."

"*Ach*, poor thing. I was too hard on her during dinner."

"She was so rude; I couldn't believe she was capable of such behavior."

Deborah started to dry the stack of dishes in front of her.

"Can I help?" Jacob asked. "Looks like we made a big mess."

Deborah turned to him and handed him her towel. "These plates need drying."

"What can I do?" Jeb asked, making his way into the kitchen.

Was it Deborah's imagination, or was Jeb competing with Jacob? He'd eaten over their place plenty of times, but never offered to wash a cup. "Jeb. Jacob. There's really no need. We have fun cleaning up."

"How could that be fun?" Jacob asked, a twinkle in his eyes.

"We talk about the men, don't you know?"

Laughter erupted in the kitchen, Uncle Isaac's soaring over the others, as he poured himself a cup of coffee. "She's right. I've been listening for years. Always get my coffee when the women folk are cleaning. *Ach*, they talk in circles."

Mary put her hands on her hips. "We do not."

"*Jah*, you do. One woman brings up a topic and it goes down the line, all women putting in their two cents, then someone starts up about something else, and around it goes."

Mary shooed Isaac out of her kitchen, and Jacob doubled over laughing.

"What's so funny?" Mary demanded to know.

Jacob put one hand up until he could breathe. "I haven't ever laughed so much. I can see we're too strict back home. It's a *gut* kind of surprise."

Deborah threw a sponge at him playfully. "Well, in this settlement, men always clean the dishes after a big meal."

Aunt Mary wagged a finger. "That's not true."

Jacob took the sponge. "It can be true for today. You women look awful tired. Go rest in the living room while Jeb and I clean up this mess."

"Seriously?" Deborah asked with a broad smile.

"*Jah*, now go on with you."

~*~

Late that night, Deborah and Mary sat up knitting scarves on their looms, while sipping hot chocolate. It was Aunt Mary's idea that they talk, and Deborah relished the time with her aunt. Most likely, she'd be going home…

"Deborah, how do you talk to your brother, Nathan?"

"With sign language. Why do you ask?"

"There's a new family that just arrived. A very large one. Thirteen *kinner*. We'll need to start a new school, of course, but one of their *kinner* is deaf."

"That's sad, but they can live normal lives with sign language. How old is he?"

"Eight, and the parents don't know this special language." She shifted in her chair. "Your Uncle Isaac and I think you'd make a *gut* teacher, and could help this little boy. What do you say?"

Deborah was planning on going back home, but not until Christmas. She did need to pitch in financially, but was it fair to the *kinner* to get attached.

"Aunt Mary, remember I said I'm homesick? I can't start teaching, and then just up and leave."

"How long would it take to teach this boy sign language?"

"A month."

"There you have it. A month teaching at the school would get your mind off your homesickness, and change a little boy's life forever. Think of the gift it would be for him to be able to learn sign language?"

Deborah put her loom down. "I accept. You're right. Time will pass and I'd be able to help a child in need."

"*Gut*. I'll tell Uncle Isaac tomorrow." She took up her loom again and knit quickly. "I think Jacob is keen on you."

Deborah rolled her eyes. "Well, he can be as keen as he wants, but I'm not apt to trust any man soon."

"Be careful. A chip on your shoulder can grow, making it hard to walk."

Deborah groaned. "I need time. Can you believe he asked me to go to a Singing?"

"What was your answer?"

"Well, Jeb was going too, so I said yes, since I know Jeb. But it was impulsive of Jacob to ask."

Aunt Mary chuckled. "*Ach*, you're going because you like Jeb."

"What?"

"And I think Jeb is keen on you, too. And Sarah's leaving. They broke-up."

Deborah's heart leapt for joy, but then plummeted down again. She barely knew Jeb, so she'd have a wall up, guarding her heart. No, she would only trust men she'd known since she was a *kinner*. She'd go home and tell Noah she'd made a mistake, and be happy to be his bride. It would be a Christmas surprise.

Like her *oma* said, her *opa* had a hard time saying he loved her, but his actions showed it. Her *opa* stayed by her side when sick. *Jeb was with her a whole day when she had a concussion. He scooped her up off the ground and ran to the house.* She quickly dismissed the thought.

"I don't *know* Jeb. Ohio is my home, and I plan to accept Noah's marriage proposal at Christmas…plain and simple…if he'll still have me. I need to write to him; tell him I've learned a lot over the past few months."

Chapter 10

Jingle Bells!

"I'm leaving today," Sarah blurted. "It's Sunday, Jacob. You're dragging your feet."

Jacob looked across the kitchen at Jeb, looking for help.

"It's winter out there. Fifty miles in an open buggy is dangerous. I think God will understand if you wait for this storm to pass. And leave in a car."

"How can you speak for God?"

"Doesn't the Bible make it clear that God is love? He cares about your safety."

When Jeb said this, he stood tall. He'd been looking for signs of God's love in hopes that the condemnation he carried would fall off like the leaves on all the trees, and it was. He saw God's love everywhere now, and chains had dropped off his neck. He'd hoped that Sarah would stay and be set free too. "Let's all sit down and have a cup of coffee. Shouting across the room was never done in my parents' house." Jeb motioned towards the oak table.

Jacob glanced at Sarah. "Sure was common in our home."

"Hush, Jacob. That's not fair to *Mamm* and *Daed*."

Jacob's shoulders slouched and he sat at the table, and Sarah did too, stiff as a board.

Jeb poured three cups of coffee from the blue speckle ware pot that made a permanent home on the woodstove, and took a seat beside Jacob, across from Sarah.

"*Mamm* and *daed* expect us to be home, Jacob. And we deceived them, saying we were coming to the auction in Smicksburg."

"I think they know now that we had other plans? We've been here several days…and we're adults."

Jeb knew this family well, and control held a high position. "I agree with Jacob. You're both grown adults." He reached for Sarah's hand, but she didn't oblige. "Sarah, is there something you see here in Smicksburg you don't see back home?"

"I do," Jacob blurted. "Smiles. Love. Folks being able to travel outside a five-mile radius by car..."

"Hush, Jacob," Sarah scolded again.

"Now look here, Sarah. I'm older than you. Stop telling me to hush-up. And I have a *gut* reason to stay in Smicksburg."

"What?" Jeb asked, hoping he wouldn't say Deborah.

"Deborah. She's what I've been looking for all my life. And she's going to the Singing with me." He looked over at Jeb. "And Jeb's going, too. How about we make it a foursome?"

Jeb moaned audibly.

"What's wrong with that?" Jacob asked.

Jeb didn't know why he kept thinking of Deborah. Preferring her over Sarah, but the thought of her being hooked up with Jacob had given him some restless nights since Thanksgiving. But he hardly knew her, and Sarah just needed to be in Smicksburg long enough...to change. Maybe she'd be as sweet as Deborah if she spent time with her.

"Sarah, please, go the Singing tonight. For me?"

Her eyes softened, and she reached across the table, taking Jeb's hand. "Jeb, you're the nicest man I know, but I just can't yield to the carnal ways of this settlement. Won't you come home?"

"Go to the Singing. Can't leave today anyhow. And you'll hear songs you've never heard."

She squeezed his hand. "Will you think about leaving with me and go back home?"

She was smiling, and not only from her lips, but her eyes. Smicksburg had rubbed off on her without her realizing it. "After the Singing, you'll want to stay."

~*~

Deborah was covered from head to toe, to keep the cold at bay. When the buggy pulled up, she went out on the porch, eager to go to the singing. Eager to see Jeb, although she'd written to Noah, pleading for forgiveness, Jeb was a *gut* friend.

Jacob jumped out of the buggy, and ran up to meet her. "Take my hand. Don't want you to slip."

"*Danki.*"

With the black side panels down on the buggy, she didn't see Jeb. What if he didn't come and it was just Jacob and herself? But as soon as she got to the buggy, she saw Jeb and flashed a smile. Then she saw Sarah, snuggled up against Jeb for warmth, and she wanted to turn and run back inside. *Why?* These silly reactions she was having concerning Jeb needed to stop. "So *gut* to see you could come, Sarah, Jeb."

"Jeb and I will be leaving to go back home to Cambria once the singing is over, and the roads are clear."

Deborah froze. She searched Jeb's eyes, and they were lifeless. Why did she want to cry all of a sudden? Tears stung her eyes, so she faked a sneeze. "I'm getting a cold. I shouldn't go."

Jacob held her hand as she descended the buggy. "I can keep you warm under the buggy robe. And we have some hot bricks too."

"I need to teach school tomorrow and can't be sick."

"You seemed fine a few seconds ago," Sarah said. "You're just upset."

"What?"

"You've tried to be my friend, and I'm thankful. But Jeb and I belong in Cambria." She snuggled closer to Jeb.

"You think I'm upset you're leaving?" Deborah couldn't believe the arrogance of this woman. Why did she think the whole world revolved around her? She needed to be honest with her. "I don't know you well, Sarah. But Jeb, he's been a *gut* friend, and I'll miss him." She slowly met Jeb's turquoise eyes. "Not many people care like Jeb does. He's an upright man and I hope he finds a wife *deserving* of him."

Sarah patted Jeb's hand. "He has already." She leaned her head on his shoulder, but Deborah continued to look into Jeb's eyes. It seemed like he was screaming for help, but it must be her imagination.

She turned and sat in the buggy. "We'll not stay late, right?"

"Home by ten. Is that okay?" Jacob pulled up the buggy robe and slid next to Deborah.

"*Jah*, that's fine."

Jacob put his arm around her. "Need to keep you warm."

"*Danki.* So, what kinds of songs are sung at a singing out here, Jeb?" Jacob asked.

"Well, from here until Christmas, Christmas Carols."

Sarah clucked her tongue. "Not hymns?"

"Well, some Carols are like hymns. They tell of the birth of Christ. How he came into the world to set us free..."

"Set us free? You're starting to sound like your radical black friend. I wish you wouldn't continue writing him."

Deborah turned and gawked at Sarah. "Carl's a *wunderbar* man. And his people really suffer."

Sarah did not meet her eyes, but stared ahead as if she hadn't even spoken. Deborah looked at Jeb, wanting an explanation.

Jeb pulled his black wool hat forward, making a shadow over his eyes. "She doesn't know Carl like we do."

"Well, he's opened up our eyes to a world we didn't know about, *jah*? Prejudice against blacks?"

Jacob started to chuckle. "*Ach*, we were raised on it. Sarah and I have a lot of unlearning to do. Sarah, don't you agree?"

Again, Sarah said nothing. Was it the wind that made her not hear the question? "Sarah, Jacob said you were raised to be prejudiced, and you need to repent."

"Repent," Sarah snarled. "For what?"

"For what? Who are you to judge another man's servant? Carl's going to be a Baptist preacher. He writes to us too, and my aunt and uncle are sending him money to help a fellow Christian in need."

"Is that right?" Jeb asked.

Sarah elbowed Jeb. "He's not German or Swiss, so how can he help our People?"

Jeb leaned away from Sarah, eyes ablaze. "Come now. We care for anyone in need, like the Good Samaritan. And we send aid around the world to orphanages and other *gut* causes. So, what's all this about not being German?"

Deborah turned around, happy that Jeb seemed to put Sarah in her place. She said a quick prayer for Jeb.

Lord,

Help him find a wife deserving of him, not someone like Sarah who will plague him all the days of his life.

~*~

Dashing through the snow
In a one horse open sleigh
O'er the fields we go
Laughing all the way
Bells on bob tails ring
Making spirits bright
What fun it is to laugh and sing
A sleighing song tonight

Oh, jingle bells, jingle bells
Jingle all the way
Oh, what fun it is to ride
In a one horse open sleigh
Jingle bells, jingle bells
Jingle all the way
Oh, what fun it is to ride
In a one horse open sleigh

Jeb clapped his hands as they sang the song faster. He met Deborah's gaze across the room. Sarah sat poker straight, and Deborah motioned towards her, a plea for help. He shrugged his shoulders, not knowing what to do. Maybe when they started slower songs, Sarah wouldn't be so nervous.

After Jingle Bells ended with hand clapping and smiles, the man who held the singing in his shop, stood up.

"Do you know the Twelve Days of Christmas?"

Many heads nodded but Jeb looked over a Jacob next to him and frowned.

"Well," the man continued, "let me read something I found interesting.

"The Partridge in a Pear Tree is Jesus Christ.

The Two Turtle Doves are the Old and New Testaments.

The Three French Hens stand for faith, hope and love.

The Four Calling Birds are the four gospels of Matthew, Mark, Luke & John.

The Five Golden rings recall the Torah or Law, the first five books of the Old Testament.

The Six Geese a-Laying stand for the six days of creation.

The Seven Swans a-Swimming represent the sevenfold gifts of the Holy Spirit–Prophesy, Serving, Teaching, Exhortation, Contribution, Leadership, and Mercy.

The Eight Maids a-Milking are the eight beatitudes.

The Nine Ladies Dancing are the nine fruits of the Holy Spirit–Love, Joy, Peace, Patience, Kindness, Goodness, Faithfulness, Gentleness, and Self Control.

The Ten Lords a-Leaping are the ten commandments.

The Eleven Pipers Piping stand for the eleven faithful disciples.

The Twelve Drummers Drumming symbolize the twelve points of belief in the Apostles' Creed."

"Isn't that something?" the man asked. In a time of Christian persecution, symbols were used by Christians so they could sing Carols without being thrown into jail." He pointed to the article as he read. "Some dispute the symbolism because they refuse to acknowledge the persecution of Catholics in England during 1558 to 1829."

Sarah shot up and made her way through the benches and out the shop door. Deborah ran after her. Jeb nudged Jacob. "We best be going."

Chapter 11

Sparks Fly

Deborah got to the schoolhouse early, surprised to see a buggy outside, and the glow of the oil lamps. When she pulled closer to the newly built little white schoolhouse, she saw a man inside, most likely the bishop to give her further instructions. But how nice of him to make a cozy fire and light all the lamps. She quickly got out of the buggy, and ran into the building since the sidewalks were clear. What a nice bishop they had.

When she opened the door, she stepped back. "Jeb. *Ach*, I expected the bishop. Are you the school superintendent?"

"*Nee*. Wanted to see you and apologize for Sarah's behavior last night. Didn't sleep a wink."

Deborah placed the books she'd bought for the *kinner* on her desk. "It wasn't your fault, Jeb."

"Well, I felt real bad. You had a bad night."

She sat in her new chair. "Sarah's prejudiced against Blacks and Catholics? I know our forefathers were persecuted by Catholics, but this is 1963."

Jeb hung his head in shame. "Well, her behavior woke me up. She's leaving and I'm staying."

Deborah clasped her hands. "Praise be."

Jeb couldn't hide a smile.

"*Ach*, my Aunt Mary says that all day long, and I'm picking up her ways. I'm really sorry for your loss." Deborah didn't know what had overcome her. As the sun rose, giving more light, she felt like her heart was lifted by this news.

"You'll be happy to know Jacob's staying though, *jah*?"

Jacob? She didn't even know him. "*Jah*, I suppose. Why isn't he going back?"

"He likes it here, and thinks he's found a reason to stay."

"And what might that be?"

Jeb grinned. "You don't know, do you?"

"What?"

"He's mighty keen on you and thinks he's found himself a wife."

Deborah broke the pencil in her hand in half. "*Ach*, how could he?"

"He said those big light blue eyes of yours encourage him. Thinks you feel the same way. Do you?"

Deborah leaned her head forward and rolled her eyes. "Jeb, why do people judge from the outside? *Jah*, I have blue eyes, as do many German people. But it says nothing about my heart. I'm sick of men asking me to marry them because of my 'light blue eyes that draw them in'. Honestly, it's a poor way to choose a wife."

"So, you've turned down other men?" Jeb sat in one of the *kinner's* chairs. "How many?"

Deborah sighed. "I've lost track."

"Lost track?"

"*Nee*, maybe five men? Or seven?" Jeb leaned his chiseled chin on his fist and stared at her. *My is he handsome today in green.* She looked down and fidgeted with the items in the top drawer of her desk. It was filled with teacher supplies.

"Compliments of Emma."

Deborah looked up at Jeb. "What?"

"Emma went out and bought all the supplies you'd need. She's a *wunderbar* woman. I hope to find someone like her someday."

Deborah licked her lips, not sure if she dare ask, but did. "So, you and Sarah are no longer courting? Not writing letters to work out your differences?"

"*Nee*. It's over. She doesn't respect me, I've come to see. And I was holding on to her for the wrong reasons. She knew my parents well, and I could talk to her about them." His voice broke and he lowered his head. "Mighty glad Carl's coming up for Christmas. A real distraction. Christmas will be hard." He slowly raised his head up. "Thanksgiving was fun at your place. How about we host Christmas?"

Deborah felt her heart burn for this man, but fear of being deceived by someone she didn't know well, soon drowned it out. "I won't be here for Christmas. You'll need to talk to my aunt."

Jeb sighed. "*Ach*, I imagined us playing Dutch Blitz and putting a puzzle together. You'll be missed. When will you come back?"

She pursed her lips. "I'm not. I'm going to accept number seven's marriage proposal."

"Come again?"

"I think Noah's the seventh man to ask, not being proud and all. I came here after I turned him down and my parents were mighty cross with me. Noah has a farm and…"

"Do you love him?" Jeb blurted.

"I can learn to, like my parents say…"

"That's *furhoodled* and you know it."

"Jebediah Weaver, I don't see that this is any of your concern."

Jeb's eyes bugged out of his head. "Just because you're mad at yourself, don't take it out on me."

"Mad at myself?"

"*Jah*. You're running away from your problems, like you did when you came out here."

"And what might that problem be?"

"You search your heart, and find out." Jeb made his way out the door.

He calls me furhoodled. He makes me furhoodled. What in the world is he talking about? Does he want me to marry Jacob?

~*~

Deborah straightened her black apron, prepared to greet her class with a smile, as *furhoodled* as she felt. There were twenty students, ranging from five to thirteen. She knew the system well, pairing *kinner* by skill and not age. She'd looked over their report cards from their former school, and after taking roll call, she told them where to sit.

Passing out Pathway Readers according to their skill levels, she asked them to silently read, while she got acquainted with Timmy. She signed '*hello. So happy to have you in my class.*'

He looked up at her, confusion written on his face.

Deborah waved at him.

He smiled and waved back.

She wrote the word, w-a-v-e on the board, and pointed to each letter and made the hand sign. Timmy seemed baffled at first, but then his eyes popped. He picked up his pencil. Deborah wrote p-e-n-c-i-l on the board, and then the sign language. To her delight, Timmy squealed with joy. He quickly raised a book up. Deborah wrote b-o-o-k and then did the sign language, and to her utter shock, Timmy ran up to her and gave her a hug.

She pat his head, warmth filling her heart. Was she called to be a teacher? She ran over to her bag of supplies and gave him a sign language chart and over the next twenty minutes, they signed many words. It appeared Timmy loved all sorts of animals, but especially dogs….and a plan started to form in her mind.

~*~

"A coon dog? You want to buy a coon dog?" Jeb and Jacob hid laughter. "Do you want to hunt with us?"

Deborah squared her shoulders. "Jebediah Weaver, you may think I'm *furhoodled*, but I'm not daft. It's for Timmy, my deaf student. He's picking up sign language quick, but he's a little high strung, not able to talk to people like we do. A pet is good for deaf *kinner*."

"*Jah*, exactly," Deborah said. "So, do you have any coon dogs for sale?"

Jeb chuckled. "Can't keep a coon dog in the house. They're born to be outside in their barrels."

"Who said?" Deborah challenged.

"You need to find a Labrador or collie. We've had both and they act more human-like."

"Where do I find such a dog?"

Abe walked into the kitchen. "Need to find a breeder, but they're expensive. Can you afford one?"

"How expensive?"

"Oh, forty dollars, for a cheap one."

Deborah held on the kitchen counter. "Forty dollars? That's two months of my pay."

"Some Amish raise Jack Russell Terriers. They're smart as a whip," Abe said. "I know of some, but they're half-breeds."

"Is that a bad thing?" Deborah asked.

"Well, can be if it's mixed with a breed not good with *kinner*. But most of the time you can tell what they're mixed with."

"Most of the time? This family has thirteen *kinner*. I need a dog that can be trusted.

"We'll find you a Lab or collie," Jeb said, bluntly, ending the conversation. He turned and headed out toward the barn.

"What's wrong with Jeb? Does he think I'm being too picky?"

Emma took her by the shoulder and led her into the living room. "He has a lot on his mind. Has someone on his mind, understand?"

"*Jah*, I do. I really do."

Emma gawked. "You do?"

Deborah nodded. "A broken heart is hard to deal with. Samuel broke mine, and it took me weeks to recover."

"*Ach*, Deborah, you don't recover from a broken heart in a week if you truly love someone."

"How do you know?"

"Because Abe broke things off with me for a year, and I never recovered until we courted again. I truly love Abe, see?"

Why was Emma telling her this? Was she trying to say Jeb would be moody for a year? Well, she'd steer clear of him if that was the case.

Jacob popped his head into the room. "Am I interrupting something?"

"Come in, Jacob" Emma said.

"Can I speak to Deborah in private?"

Emma grinned. "*Jah*, for sure."

Jacob came in a took a seat in a rocker. "Sit down, Deborah. Relax."

She obeyed, but hoped he wasn't going to ask her to go out on a buggy ride, because the answer was no.

"I can tell if a Jack Russell's mixed with an aggressive dog. And the farm up the road has a few pups. Want to go take a look?"

Deborah's mouth parted, not expecting such tenderness. "*Jah*, I'd like to see them."

Chapter 12

Love?

Jeb stabbed the hay with a pitchfork. Deborah was leaving, and he had to accept it. She would wed a man she didn't love. But she gave no indication that if someone showed her attention, she'd give her heart to another.

He'd come to realize he'd never loved Sarah, after he met Deborah. Well, at first she'd rubbed him the wrong way, for sure and for certain, but his rough ways were chipped off by her. And she hung on every word he said pertaining to scripture. And now, she was memorizing large passages. And she, along with Abe and Emma, had introduced him to poetry, especially Robert Frost. Emma's idea for him to buy Frost's new book, *In the Clearing*, for Deborah was too forward. Anyhow, she could read their copy.

*Women love presents...*It was something his *mamm* always said. How she'd brighten when his *daed* would bring home something for her, even a trifle, like a box of chocolates.

His parents. How would he get through Christmas without them…and Deborah? His chin quivered and he waved a fist in the air.

Lord, I need your help. It's too much to bear. Just thinking of Christmas makes it hard to breathe. I miss them so. Why did you take them? Why?

Soon, tears streamed down his cheeks and he let them fall. The more he read the Bible, knowing God wanted a relationship and King David talked honestly to God, reasoned with him, he knew to pray from a sincere heart with sincere questions wasn't a sin.

He bowed his head to continue this conversation with the Lord, but heard someone clear his voice. It was Jacob, with Deborah by his side.

"Jeb, you okay?"

"*Jah*, I'm fine."

"You're sobbing. You miss Sarah that much?" Jacob asked.

"*Nee*. Not really. It's my parents. The holidays were special." He wiped his eyes, and even though his chin was still shaking, he asked, "Do you want something?"

"The buggy. Deborah and I are going for a ride."

He put his head down to hide his pain. "Have a *gut* time."

~*~

Deborah was glad to get home to her Aunt Mary's house. Her Uncle Isaac greeted her with a warm embrace. "Never seem to see my niece. How was school today?"

"*Gut*. Real *gut*. And I met Timmy, the boy who's deaf. I'm really taken with him."

Uncle Isaac rubbed the top of her head as if she was a *kinner*. "That's *gut*. I knew you had the makings of a teacher."

"You did?"

"*Jah*. You're using your God given talents and I'm thinking He's happy about that."

If she left, would she be neglecting this talent? Maybe she was to be an old maidel school teacher. Saint Paul was single and in Corinthians he said being single was a good thing

Sitting her books down on the table, she scooped up stew that was set on the stove. "Sorry I missed supper. Trying to find a dog for Timmy. Deaf children do better with a dog."

"And I'm sure you asked his parents?"

"*Jah*, of course. But a *gut* dog is expensive. Forty dollars."

"Land's sakes. You can buy a cheap horse for that price. How about a mutt."

"Some are mixed with mean dogs, and with them having a *boppli*, I just don't know."

Aunt Mary came into the kitchen, eyes aglow. "You received a letter from back home."

"*Danki*." She kissed her aunt's cheek. "And that's for the stew. I'm sorry I can't help."

"You're a teacher now."

"But I miss being in the kitchen already." She looked down at the letter. The return address was Noah's. Her appetite vanished, and she asked to be excused to read the letter.

Taking a seat in the living room, she opened the letter.

Deborah,

I received your letter and accept your apology. Maybe the good people in Smicksburg have made you see reason. A home is built by hard work, one board at a time, like I said. You're probably seeing this in your aunt and uncle's home. Love isn't a feeling; it's a commitment. The proposal still stands, if you're willing to work hard and build a marriage and home with me.

Noah

She scanned the letter for some secret meaning. Some softness. But it appeared that he was scolding her. As for her aunt and uncle, love didn't seem like hard work at all.

Her aunt entered the room. "Is it good news?"

"I don't know. Aunt Mary, I'm confused. Can you read this?"

"It's addressed to you."

"Please."

Aunt Mary took the letter and sat in her rocker. When she'd read it, she gawked. "Deborah, marriage is work, but not slave labor."

"What do you mean?"

"He's asking you to go into a loveless marriage. I've read letters from satisfied customers with more feeling. *Ach*, you deserve better."

"But many Amish marry and love comes. It's a commitment."

"Deborah, I know you. You have a sensitive nature. I'm not saying weak, but sensitive. Look at nature. Roses are sensitive, needing lots of attention. I see you as a rose. A rose that would wither and die under Noah's care."

"How do you know?"

"I'm a rose, too. And you see how your uncle treats me. With tender loving care."

Deborah lowered her head. "I don't want to be an old *maidel*."

"You're twenty-one and still young. The right man will come along and you'll know."

"How?"

"You'll blossom.

Deborah knew what she needed to do. Write to Noah and turn him down, again. And she wouldn't be going home for Christmas, not able to face her parents, especially her *daed*. What if the news made his heart condition worse?

~*~

A few days later, while Deborah was in the middle of a Spelling Bee, the door to the schoolhouse flew open, and one of the parents blew in. "Deborah you're needed," he blurted.

"What's the matter? Deborah asked.

"An accident. Men cutting ice and some went under."

"Where?"

"Over at the Weaver's. I need women to help nurse the sick."

Deborah tried to focus but the room started to spin. "Was anyone seriously hurt?"

"*Jah*, Jeb. He tried to rescue people and got pulled under."

"And?" Deborah screamed.

"He's suffering from hypothermia mighty bad. Hope pneumonia doesn't set in."

Deborah dismissed the class, knowing the weather was milder than usual and all the kids walked.

She grabbed her cape and ran to her buggy to see Jeb. *Lord, don't take Jeb. I need him.*

~*~

Deborah took Jeb's stone-cold hand and rubbed it. His fever was at 104 last check and he wasn't waking up, no matter how hard they tried. When the room was clear, she let out a sob. "Jeb, don't leave me. Wake up!"

She heard voices and the doctor soon came into the room. After taking Jeb's pulse, he gave him another dose of penicillin.

"Will that help? Deborah asked.

"Let's hope for the best…."

Deborah remembered what Jeb said about fresh air. "Jeb's sister had tuberculosis and slept outside even in winter. Jeb said it helped her recover."

The doctor shook his head. "He needs to be kept warm…"

"Are you sure? I mean," a sob escaped, "he won't die, will he?"

"Are you his wife?"

"*Nee*, a friend."

"Well, he'll need to be watched around the clock. Keep him warm, lots of liquids."

"Isn't there any other medicine? An herb to be used?"

"Penicillin is all we have. Something new will be available soon, but – "

"What?" Can we get it?"

"A thing called antibiotics. Some feel that pneumonia is caused by a bacterial infection, and this new medicine will fight bacteria."

"Garlic does right now. Can we give him some? My *mamm* makes garlic tea with honey…"

"If he'll swallow it," the doctor said with a smile. "Give it a try. Can't hurt."

When the doctor left, Deborah continued to try to get Jeb to wake up, to no avail.

~*~

Jeb shook his head, one eye open. Deborah forced a spoonful of garlic tea into his mouth, and he spit it out.

"Jebediah Weaver, you stubborn man. This is *gut* medicine."

He opened the other eye and stared at her, but no words were spoken.

"Please, Jeb. Take this tea…for me." Another sob escaped. "You're mighty sick, and my *mamm* made us take this. Please?"

His eyes filled with tears and he opened his mouth, allowing her to put a spoonful of garlic tea in.

He reached for her hand. "*Mamm*? Miss you."

Deborah's heart raced. He was talking and his fever had come down over the night to 102. No amount of coaxing from Abe and Emma, and especially Jacob, would not make her move from Jeb's side.

He risked his life, saving her Uncle Isaac, and she was so grateful. But she knew it was more than that. How she reacted when hearing of the accident was revealing. She didn't think of anyone else's safety, except Jeb's. Her *oma* was right, anyone can act, but a reaction tells the truth.

He reached for her hand. "*Daed*. Is he here?"

"*Jah*, in the next room. He's fine."

"Is Deborah here?"

She pursed her lips together as tears streamed down her cheeks. "*Jah*, she's here, too."

A faint smile lifted his face. "A darling."

Deborah couldn't only choke on tears, not able to speak.

"*Mamm*, don't …cry"

She took a deep breath. "I have a cold, is all."

His eyes were filled with love. How he must have loved his *mamm*…cherished her…her *oma* always said to watch how a man treats his *mamm*…that's how he'll treat his wife.

Fear about trusting a man seemed to release from her heart naturally. She loved Jebediah Weaver. But did he love her?

Chapter 13

~~~

Two Candles Shine Brighter

Deborah fell asleep in the chair, the teapot of garlic tea resting in her lap. Jeb woke up, not knowing why she was in his bedroom. Was she like Ruth in the Bible, sitting at the feet of Boaz, making it clear she wanted to be his wife? Jeb sat up and took the pot from her hands, but he startled her and she woke up, eyes as round as saucers. "*Ach*, you're alive."

"Of course, I'm alive."

Deborah ran out of the room to get Emma, and soon the whole family was in his room. Was he dreaming? What was going on?"

Abe bent down to hug him, eyes brimming with tears. Emma did the same in turn as did Jacob.

"You sure had us scared," Abe blurted.

"Scared? Why?"

"You've been in bed for a week. Remember cutting ice, and the accident?"

Jeb's brows furrowed. "Not really."

"Well, you saved some people's lives, but almost got yourself killed."

Jeb laid his head back on the pillow and closed his eyes. "Anyone die?"

"*Nee*, but I could have, if it hadn't been for you." Abe let tears run down his cheeks and into his beard.

"And my Uncle Isaac, too," Deborah said.

Jeb opened his eyes, filled with sorrow. "So, I didn't see her."

"Who?" Emma asked.

"My *mamm*. I had a dream that I was talking with her. We had long talks."

Abe sat at the foot of Jeb's bed, and took his brother's hand. "You were talking to Deborah. She nursed you back to health. Refused to leave your side."

Jeb looked over at Deborah, and her light blue eyes were filled with love; the kind of love a woman has for a man. But most likely, he was still suffering from delirium, because she was going to leave and wed someone else in Ohio. "*Danki*, Deborah. I'll miss you…" Tears ran from the sides of his eyes and on to his pillow."

"I'm not going anywhere…"

"Not today, but in time."

She smiled at him with such warmth, he knew he was dreaming.

~*~

Deborah always loved the many garlands and candles that adorned the one-room schoolhouse when she was a *kinner*, and so she took the whole day on Saturday to decorate. Although it was usually a group activity, she craved solitude. Having been at the Weavers for a week, and not knowing if Jeb would make it had taken its toll. She slept for two days straight when she arrived back home.

Taking branches of evergreen with red berries, she placed them along the ledges of each window sill. When all ten windows were done, she took the red tapered candles and placing them all in glass holders, she put two in each window, since there were twenty in the box.

When finished, she looked around the room, but it didn't have the effect she wanted. Evergreens needed to be tacked all around the window, framing it. There just wasn't enough color in the room.

Going over to her art supplies, she got red and green colored paper and started to cut strips to make a paper chain.

Her mind wandered toward Jebediah Weaver more often than she liked. One of the fruits of the Spirit was self-control, so to not be able to stop thinking about someone wasn't right.

But she missed him, not able to come back to work, the doctor afraid he might have a relapse. But when she took over meals, he seemed flushed. Most likely, still feverish. She thought of 1 Corinthians 13, as she now had it memorized. Jeb was everything, that love should be: patient, kind, not rude, not seeking his own way…he even laid his life down for a friend, which the Bible said was the greatest love. If it hadn't been for Jeb, she might be attending Uncle Isaac and Abe's funerals. Emma and Aunt Mary might be widows…

She knew word got out to Cambria County about Jeb's condition, because letters by the basketful were delivered to his home. Was he in touch with Sarah again? Her heart ached, because she now knew what love was. She'd marry Jebediah Weaver if he asked. *If* he'd ask.

She heard a dog barking. No, crying outside. Since she had a roaring fire in the woodstove, she'd let the poor thing in and warm up. But then she heard a knock. Dogs don't knock. Was it a student wanting to talk to her? A crying student. *Ach*, she was a teacher Monday through Friday and needed the day off.

She slowly went to the door, and upon opening it a yellow Lab, with a red bow around his neck ran to her, his big brown eyes begged for attention. "Uncle Isaac, come in. I know it's you. Honestly, you spoil me like a *kinner*."

Uncle Isaac didn't come in, but Jeb Weaver did. Flustered, she blurted, "So my uncle had you deliver him?"

Jeb adjusted his black wool hat. "What?"

"I went on and on about yellow Labs, trying to find one for Timmy. He must have spent a week's wages on this pup."

Jeb took off his hat and walked over to the woodstove to rub his hands. "I got the dog. I'm awfully obliged to you for nursing me back to health. And your uncle did mention you wanted one for yourself."

"*Ach*, but these dogs are so expensive, Jeb...."

"I got a ride back to Cambria County because I knew of a family that breeds them. Sells them real cheap."

Deborah knelt and nuzzled the fur against her face to hide the tears that threatened to spill over. *Did Jeb care for her?* "*Danki*, Jeb. But I'll be giving him to Timmy."

"I got one for him too."

"You did? *Ach*, Jeb. How did he react?"

"Don't know. Wanted to surprise you first." He looked around the schoolhouse, reached up and fidgeting with the brim on his black hat that was sprinkled with snow. "Looks real nice in here. We never decorated our schoolhouses for Christmas. This is nice."

Deborah continued to pet the dog to calm herself. *Does Jeb care for me?* "We had evergreens all around the windows, but I can't reach the top."

Jeb went over and put his hand up against the top of the window. "I can. Let me help."

"*Ach, danki*, Jeb. And I can help you."

"How? Get up on a chair?" Jeb winked.

Again, heat rose in Deborah's face. "I'll hand you the tacks when you're ready."

A broad smile slid across his face. "Teamwork, then. I think we'd make a *gut* team."

They gathered up branches and headed towards the window near the door. "So, how was your visit to Cambria?" Deborah immediately braced herself to hear Jeb say that he and Sarah got things worked out.

Jeb tacked an evergreen in place. "Painful."

"Why?"

"Put the farm up for sale."

"So, you won't be going back?"

"*Nee*, Smicksburg's my home now."

"And Sarah? Will she move here?"

He put another branch in place and when Deborah handed him a tack, he held her hand. "*Nee*, Sarah won't be coming here."

"She won't?" Deborah held Jeb's gaze.

"*Nee.*" He drew her to himself. "I love you Deborah, and I'm praying to God I'm not number eight."

Deborah felt her heart race. *He loves me? Praise be!*

"I know you've turned down seven proposals, and I fear I may be the eighth. But let me explain why you should accept."

Deborah felt like she was in a dream and blurted out, "Yes!"

He got down on one knee, now being eye-level with Deborah. "I'm a hard worker and you'll want for nothing."

"*Jah!*"

"And I've never loved anyone before, really. So, you have my heart."

"*Jah!*"

Jeb narrowed his eyes. "What do you mean? That I'll be a hard worker or that I'll love you forever."

Deborah cupped his hands around his face. "*Jah*, I'll marry you."

Jeb sprang up and twirled her around. "Deborah, I've loved you for so long." He bent down to kiss her tenderly on the lips.

Over and over in her mind, Deborah kept thinking, *Praise be! I found a man I can trust and truly love.*

Jeb reached into his pocket for his matches, and lit the two candles in the window. "There's more light with two candles. More joy." He picked her up and kissed her again.

She held on to him and couldn't stop smiling for joy. "I could never find anyone I wanted to grow old with, until I met you."

Chapter 14

A Merry Christmas

Abe looked around at everyone at the table as the turkey and trimming stayed warm in the oven. "Carl, so *gut* to have you with us today."

Carl tugged on the red scarf Deborah had made for him for Christmas, and looked over at her beaming. "Didn't think I'd be having Christmas in a white house." He nudged Jeb who sat next to him? "Remember when I was afraid to go into a house full of whites?"

"*Jah*, I sure do," Jeb said.

Abe handed the black Bible to Carl. "Can you read the scripture pertaining to Christ's birth? Will you read?"

Carl nodded, and then flashed a smile around the table.

And it came to pass in those days, that there went out a decree from Caesar Augustus that all the world should be taxed.

And Joseph also went up from Galilee, out of the city of Nazareth, into Judaea, unto the city of David, which is called Bethlehem; (because he was of the house and lineage of David:)

To be taxed with Mary his espoused wife, being great with child.

And so it was, that, while they were there, the days were accomplished that she should be delivered.

And she brought forth her firstborn son, and wrapped him in swaddling clothes, and laid him in a manger; because there was no room for them in the inn.

And there were in the same country shepherds abiding in the field, keeping watch over their flock by night.

And, lo, the angel of the Lord came upon them, and the glory of the Lord shone round about them: and they were sore afraid.

And the angel said unto them, Fear not: for, behold, I bring you good tidings of great joy, which shall be to all people.

For unto you is born this day in the city of David a Savior, which is Christ the Lord.

And this shall be a sign unto you; Ye shall find the babe wrapped in swaddling clothes, lying in a manger.

And suddenly there was with the angel a multitude of the heavenly host praising God, and saying,

Glory to God in the highest, and on earth peace, good will toward men.

And it came to pass, as the angels were gone away from them into heaven, the shepherds said one to another, Let us now go even unto Bethlehem, and see this thing which is come to pass, which the Lord hath made known unto us.

Abe asked if anyone would like to say the blessing, and Aunt Mary put her hand up. "I want to say a word of *thanks*." Her eyes fell on Jeb and Deborah, who sat side by side on the bench. "I'd like to thank God that my niece got back on the straight and narrow by her friendship with Jeb."

All eyes went on Deborah, and she feared she was blushing, or the room was mighty hot. "Well, I still want a clothes dryer, but some things aren't worth losing my Amish heritage and community over. And, truth be told, I do like to hang the wash out, when it's not cold." She wrung her hands, trying to hide them under the table. "All these modern conveniences should be accepted or rejected as a community."

Emma said she had a word of thanks, too. "I want to thank God that Jeb has learned more about the love of God from his friendship with Deborah."

Deborah looked at Jeb, puzzled. "Did you tell them?"

"*Nee*, I said nothing."

Aunt Mary laughed. "Isaac, the school superintendent went to check on the schoolhouse. Saw smoke and it being Saturday, knew the school was closed." He covered her mouth to hide a grin. "He saw you two kissing by the window."

Deborah cupped her cheeks. "*Ach*, now it won't be a surprise, come next November."

"Next November?" Jeb asked. "Why not get married sooner. How about Old Christmas?"

Deborah spun her head up at him. "My folks are in Ohio and winter travel is dangerous, *jah?*"

"Not in a car," Jeb said with a wink.

Aunt Mary clasped her hands. "We can have it at our place. My *kinner* will be home – "

Uncle Isaac stood up. "I can't take it anymore. I'm starving. You all can make wedding plans after we eat."

Laughter made its way around the room, and Deborah felt such warmth in her heart, she didn't know how to contain her happiness. But to get married in a few weeks? She loved Jebediah Weaver with all her heart, something she didn't think possible. But a wedding now? *Lord, help!*

Chapter 15

Wedding Plans

The next day, on Second Christmas, Jeb pulled the buggy robe up higher. "Are you warm enough?"

"*Jah*, I am. The hot bricks help." Deborah snuggled up closer to him. Jeb put his arm around her and pulled into the road leading to the one-room schoolhouse.

Through chattering teeth, Deborah asked why he was headed towards the school since it was closed. "It's a surprise," Jeb said, stealing a kiss from her soft cheek. "You're sure about marrying me, *jah*?"

"*Jah*. No doubts."

"Well, I don't either."

"You're over Sarah, completely?"

A gust of wind blew so hard, Jeb had to hold on to his black wool hat. "Completely. She lacked something. A mind of her own."

"Well, my *daed* says that's my shortcoming…"

"*Nee.* Like I said, I want to know what goes on in my wife's mind, not having to guess." He snickered. "So, you're an answer to prayer."

She leaned her head on his shoulder. "And I always wanted a strict Amish man, but one with a kind heart. And that's you."

As he pulled the sleigh up to the schoolhouse, she saw the red candles in the windows, and remembered their kiss. *Ach, I'll marry him on Old Christmas if he wants to.*

He held out his hand to help her out of the sleigh, and together they walked up the walkway. "Who shoveled the snow? And why so many footprints?"

Jeb only smiled and opened the door. When she entered, the schoolhouse was full of beautifully arranged flower, mostly wildflowers. The scent took her home, to her *oma*, her childhood. Tears welled in her eyes. "*Ach*, Jeb, whatever for?"

He took her hands and led her to her desk chair. He opened the Robert Frost book she got him for Christmas and read:

"The Prayer of Spring

Oh, give us pleasure in the flowers today;
And give us not to think so far away
As the uncertain harvest; keep us here
All simply in the springing of the year."

He got down on one knee and took Deborah's hand. "I bought your spring for Christmas. I've come a long way, *jah*? Thinking flowers showed pride?"

Deborah could hardly breathe, so touched by the beauty around her…and before her. *Jeb*. She threw her arms around him. "I'll marry you, today, on Old Christmas, Jeb."

"What?"

"All my talk yesterday about having a spring wedding. I was *furhoodled*. Let's marry today. This place is beautiful…"

Jeb stroked her petite hand. "Love is patient. I won't be impulsive." He stood up, scooping her into his arms. "*Nee*, Deborah Byler, you will have the wedding you've dreamed of. In the early spring with flowers all around you."

"But not back in Millersburg, but here. I'm at home here. My heart is here, with you."

Jeb looked at the poem again. "*Give us pleasure in the flowers today; And give us not to think so far away...*

She gladly accepted the kiss he planted on her lips...and the plan to marry in God's good time, and not think so far away. He had bought her spring in winter; she had a feeling he'd fill her heart with spring all year long for many years.

Dear Readers,

I hope you liked *Amish Knitting Circle Christmas*. A big thank you to an Amish woman who shared with me about the new Smicksburg Amish settlement that started in 1963, most settlers coming from Millersburg, Ohio. From what I've seen, the Amish of Smicksburg are the kindest of all Amish settlements I've been to, and I hope I portrayed the new settlement realistically. Like I always say, Smicksburg is my little slice of heaven on earth.

In all my books, I leave you with a recipe. The two recipes below are from Emma Kinsinger, an Old Order Mennonite woman who lost her husband in a construction accident in Pittsburgh, leaving her to raise ten children. I asked Emma to write a memorial to Melvin, her dearly loved husband. Here's the memorial, and Melvin's two favorite Christmas dishes.

In memory of my loving husband Melvin Kinsinger.

As Christmas approaches I automatically think of two of his favorite foods. He didn't mind what was on the menu as long as the main course included sage dressing and there was peanut butter pie for dessert.

This year as the children and I will prepare his favorite meal of the year it won't seem right without hearing him ask the blessing and making a special note to thank God for the salvation he provided. We will eat his favorite food and reflect on his Godly example and direction he left for us.

Sage Dressing

5 cup bread cubes

1/2 stick butter

1 small onion diced

2 cups chicken broth

1/2 tsps. black pepper

1/2 tsps. salt

1/4 tsps. powdered sage

In a skillet sauté onion in butter until tender and golden. Add chicken broth and seasonings. Pour over bread cubes. Use to stuff turkey or simply bake in a casserole dish at 375 for 45 minutes.

Peanut Butter Pie

2 cup milk (divided)

1/2 cup sugar (divided)

2 egg yolks beaten

1/4 cup cornstarch

1 tsp. vanilla

1/2 tsp. salt

2 Tbsp. butter

Heat 1-1/2 cup milk and half of the sugar. Mix beaten egg yolk and remaining sugar. Set aside. Mix remaining milk and cornstarch. Add egg mixture and stir. Pour into heated milk and bring to boil. Stir constantly. Boil until thick. Remove from heat and add salt, butter and vanilla. Cool completely.

Mix 3/4 cup powdered sugar and 1/2 cup peanut butter until uniformly crumbly. Spread 3/4 of it in the bottom of a pre-bakes pie shell. Add cooled pudding. Top with 1 container of cool whip and sprinkle remaining peanut butter crumbs on top.

About Author Karen Anna Vogel

Karen Anna Vogel has worn many hats: stay-at-home mom to four kids, home school vet, entrepreneur substitute teacher (aka survivor) wife to Tim for 36 years, musician. Writing has always been a constant passion, so Karen was thrilled to meet her literary agent, Joyce Hart, in a bookstore...gabbing about Amish fiction.

After her kids flew the coop, she delved into writing, and a dozen or more books later, she's passionate about portraying the Amish and small-town life in a realistic way, many of her novels based on true stores. Living in rural, PA, she writes about all the beauty around her: rolling hills, farmland, the sound of buggy wheels.

She's a graduate from Seton Hill University (psychology & education) and Andersonville Theological Seminary (Masters in Biblical Counseling). In her spare time, she enjoys knitting, photography, homesteading, and sitting around bonfires with family and friends. You can send her a message at www.karenannavogel.com/contact

Karen's booklist so far (2017)
Check her author page on Amazon for updates

Continuing Series:
Amish Knitting Circle: Smicksburg Tales 1
Amish Knitting Circle: Smicksburg Tales 2
Amish Knit Lit Circle: Smicksburg Tales 3
Amish Knit & Stitch Circle: Smicksburg Tales 4
Amish Knit & Crochet Circle: Smicksburg 5

Standalone Novels:
Knit Together: Amish Knitting Novel
The Amish Doll: Amish Knitting Novel
Plain Jane: A Punxsutawney Amish Novel

Amish Herb Shop Series:
Herbalist's Daughter Trilogy
Herbalist's Son Trilogy

Novellas:
Amish Knitting Circle Christmas: Granny & Jeb's Love Story
Amish Pen Pals: Rachael's Confession
Christmas Union: Quaker Abolitionist of Chester County, PA
Love Came Down at Christmas
Love Came Down at Christmas 2

Non-fiction:
31 Days to a Simple Life the Amish Way
A Simple Christmas the Amish Way

Karen Anna Vogel

Amish Knitting Circle Christmas

Karen Anna Vogel

Printed in Great Britain
by Amazon